Croatia

Front cover: Korčula

Right: Sculpture of Bishop Grgur of Nin
by Ivan Meštrović in Split

TOP 10 ATTRACTIONS

Basilica of Euphrasius in Poreč The mosaics here are superb examples of Byzantine art *(page 47)*

Dubrovnik This stunning city has been dubbed the 'Pearl of the Adriatic' *(page 70)*

Rab Town •
A quintessential coastal town is found on the island of Rab *(page 58)*

Tvrđa The old quarter of Osijek has fine baroque architecture *(page 39)*

Roman Amphitheatre in Pula Once known as Polensium, the city is home to Croatia's top archaeological site *(page 42)*

Cylindrical St Donat's Just one of several fine churches in Zadar *(page 61)*

Diocletian's Palace A remarkably intact Roman complex in Split *(page 66)*

Plitvice Lakes National Park Comprises a chain of 16 lakes linked by waterfalls *(page 36)*

Paklenica National Park Popular for climbing and hiking *(page 56)*

Mljet National Park in Southern Dalmatia With two stunning lakes, Mljet reflects the beauty of Croatia's coastline *(page 79)*

CONTENTS

74

91

41

57

32
53

INTRODUCTION

Croatia may be one of Europe's newest nations, only gaining its independence in a bloody divorce from Yugoslavia in 1991, but it has already emerged as one of the world's most alluring tourist destinations. Its small size, just 56,538 sq km (21,824 sq miles), is deceptive, as packed into this boomerang-shaped country is an incredible variety of scenery, from the magnificent 1,778km- (1,105 mile-) long coastline to the lofty mountains and sweeping fertile plains of the interior. Across the Adriatic from Italy, and bordered by Slovenia, Hungary, Serbia, Bosnia-Herzegovina and Montenegro, the country is at a political and ethnic crossroads that has shaped its identity.

A Natural Playground

Croatia's most dramatic natural attraction is its Adriatic coastline, which sweeps from Slovenia in the north to the Montenegrin border in the south, taking in 1,185 islands en route. Crystal clear water and countless bays and coves lure visitors and locals alike. In summer the climate is glorious, with hot sunny days tempered by a cooling breeze that eases in off the Adriatic. Even in the spring and autumn the mercury usually rises high enough to allow T-shirts to be worn during the day.

Away from the beaches massive mountain ranges such as the Učka, Biokovo and Velebit offer opportunities for hiking, climbing and extreme sports. Further inland there is the Plitvice Lakes National Park, a limestone oasis of gushing streams, pounding waterfalls and green-hued lakes that is a

UNESCO sites

UNESCO has listed six World Heritage Sites in Croatia: Dubrovnik, Diocletian's Palace in Split, the Plitvice Lakes, the Euphrasian Basilica in Poreč, Trogir and Šibenik Cathedral.

UNESCO World Heritage Site. Less visited by tourists but in its own way just as impressive is the Krka National Park in Dalmatia, with a series of lakes and streams plunging inexorably towards the Adriatic in a dramatic passage through the karst backbone of the country.

Croatia's varied landscape also makes it an oasis for sports enthusiasts and lovers of the outdoors. It is a popular destination for sailing, as recognised by millionaires such as Bill Gates, who bring their opulent yachts to cruise around the islands. This new breed of luxury traveller is catered for by an increasing number of chic restaurants and hotels that are a far cry from the faceless concrete blocks that kicked off Croatian tourism in the 1960s.

The sailors now flocking to the 50 marinas that dot the coastline are increasingly being joined by scuba divers. Conditions are excellent for diving, with a range of sites suitable for divers of all levels. The island of Biševo with its famous Blue Grotto is every bit as alluring as its Italian counterpart in Capri, and around the neighbouring island of Vis there are at least a dozen shipwrecks suitable for diving. All along the coast there are diving schools where novices can make their first dive and the more experienced can organise explorations of one of the least spoilt diving destinations in Europe.

Blue Flag Beaches

Croatia may not have the fine sandy beaches that you find in Italy and Spain, but it does have some of the cleanest beaches anywhere in Europe. There are more than 100 Blue Flag beaches dotted along the coastline. The Blue Flag is awarded by the European Union as a recognition of cleanliness, something that the authorities are keen to ensure through their conservation programmes. For a full list of Croatia's Blue Flag beaches see <www.blueflag.org>.

Dubrovnik, one of the most beautiful cities in Europe

Cities and Towns

As well as eight national parks, Croatia's towns and cities also hold plenty of interest, with the capital and most populous city Zagreb a large, increasingly modern metropolis complete with high-class hotels, richly stocked museums and restaurants that reflect its cosmopolitan nature. To the south, the Austrian-Hungarian architectural and political influences of Zagreb and Varaždin give way on the coast to Venetian and Roman remnants.

Split, Croatia's second largest city, is a chaotic, sprawling centre built on the shores of the Adriatic with its core housed inside the 2,000-year-old Diocletian's Palace. This World Heritage city-within-a-city is bursting with bars, cafés and boutiques that are all wrapped up in a Mediterranean buzz. Every city, town and village in Croatia has something to recommend it, not least the depth of history that comes from a country where the Greeks, Romans, French, Venetians and Hungarians have all vied for control over the centuries. The legacy of this eclectic past is evident in world-class attractions such as the 2,000-year-old Roman Arena in Pula and the mosaic-embellished Basilica of Euphrasius in Poreč, another World Heritage site, but it also surfaces when you least expect it, when a Venetian belltower emerges above an insignificant town or when you come upon an arrow-straight thoroughfare that has been smoothed over by Roman sandals.

Croatia also has its own home-grown architectural highlights such as Šibenik and the most striking town of them all, Dubrovnik. This self-styled 'Pearl of the Adriatic' is stunning, a complete city-state that has been immaculately preserved in its original baroque glory. Walking around Dubrovnik during the renowned summer festival or savouring the sun melting into the Adriatic from its ramparts are unforgettable experiences.

Café culture in Dubrovnik

A Split Personality

The locals of Zagreb and Split live very different lives that hint at the contrast between the two main cultures in Croatia: the Central European order and rationality of the north and the more laid-back lifestyle of the

Holy folk

Croatians are devout Roman Catholics and since independence the country has received three papal visits. The minority of ethnic Serbs in the country are Orthodox.

coast, where the steamy summer days slow things down and necessitate the siestas that are anathema to the hard-working citizens of Zagreb. In the capital they talk of their coastal brethren as being lazy, while in Split, where people pride themselves on their chic sense of style and sophistication, Zagreb is dismissed as being dull and uptight. It is a rivalry that ripples through the nation. Bring the Serbs of Krajina, the Bosnians of the border areas and the Slovenian influences of the northwest into the mix and more contrasting lifestyles emerge, with the varying ways of life co-existing today in relative harmony.

Don't Mention the War

Despite what the national tourist office may hope, it is difficult to write about Croatia without mentioning 'the war'. Images of a burning Dubrovnik and helpless refugees filled TV screens across the world in the early 1990s. However, the reality is that, except in a few places such as Vukovar and Knin, it is hard to tell that the bitter conflict ever burned through the country. Indeed it is perhaps the years of communism combined with the Homeland War that have kept Dubrovnik, its riviera and Croatia's other treasures unspoilt for so long. It is only when you make a conscious effort to search for clues, such as differently coloured roof tiles and strangely quiet villages, that the scars emerge. For those interested in what happened, many locals are only too keen to talk to anyone showing an interest in a conflict that some Croats still feel the rest of Europe did not do enough to prevent or to bring to an end.

Croatia Today

The war is rapidly fading into history as younger Croats are growing up with no recollection of what happened in the darkest days of 1991. Croatia may only have finally got back all of its territory in 1998, but the country has made rapid progress in putting itself on the map, not least with international sporting successes (see page 22). Major tour operators have returned to the country and budget air-travel routes are growing.

Choir boys in Split

Croatia's post-war progress was partially put on hold by the controversial right-wing president Franjo Tudjman, but after his death in 1999 the country was welcomed into the global fold. In addition, Croatia's willingness to hand over war criminals to the Hague has improved its status abroad. Croatia now hopes to become part of the European Union by 2010. This recognition would seal a dramatic rise from a war-torn corner of Yugoslavia into a modern European nation, with a positive and optimistic outlook, that is also one of Europe's most beautiful tourist destinations.

A BRIEF HISTORY

Delving into the complex history of one of Europe's youngest nations throws up as many unresolved questions as it does answers. Croatia has only really been an independent nation on three occasions: during the reign of the Croatian kings in the 10th and 11th centuries, during World War II, though it was essentially a Nazi puppet state, and since 1991 after its bitter divorce from Yugoslavia. Most Croats today have always felt a strong sense of national identity despite previously being labelled as Yugoslav on their passports, which makes gleaning unbiased historical information from within the country a tricky task.

From Prehistory

Thanks to the discovery of 'Krapina Man' and his Neanderthal kinsmen in the Zagorje region *(see page 34)* in the 19th century, it has been possible to trace habitation in Croatia to 30,000BC. The hilltop settlement where the remains were found, near the small town of Krapina, is one of the most important prehistoric sites in Europe. Along the Croatian coast there is also a scattering of evidence that hunter-gatherers may have settled in the region at least 20,000 years ago.

Greeks, Romans and Byzantines

By the time the Greeks arrived on the island of Vis in the 4th century BC, a smattering of tribes known as the Illyrians inhabited both the coastal areas and hinterland. From 229BC on-

Emperor Diocletian

The Roman emperor Diocletian was born in Salona (near Split). Upon retirement in around AD300 he returned to his roots and built a vast palace, which still stands today.

wards the Romans moved into the region, rapidly swallowing up large chunks of the country and beginning their makeover by building solid roads and structured towns, and imposing their way of life. The amphitheatre in Pula *(see page 42)* dates from this period, as does Diocletian's Palace in Split *(see page 66)*. Many other reminders of Roman heritage can be seen in Croatia today.

The Romans continued to hold sway over the region until the western part of their empire collapsed in the 5th century. For a short time Croatia was ruled by the Ostrogoths, before the eastern part of the Roman Empire, known as Byzantium, gained control of Istria and Dalmatia. The dominance of the first few centuries of Roman rule never truly returned, with persistent threats both from the Illyrians and the Asian Avars.

Croatia's Kings

The Croats are widely thought to be a Slavic people who came to the region in a mass migration from the plains to the north. Their Slavic cousins, the Serbs and Slovenes, are also thought to have moved to the area around this time. As

Bronze of Grgur of Nin, by the sculptor Ivan Meštrović

more Croats arrived their influence grew and they acquired their own king, Tomislav, a heroic character still revered in Croatia. In securing the Croatian state in 925, Tomislav saw off both the Venetian Republic and the Hungarians. Following the end of Tomislav's reign in 928 a succession of kings took their turn as the Croatian monarch, but Tomislav remains the symbolic hero.

The emblematic Lion of Venice on a church in Istria

It was during this period that Croats began converting to Christianity. Recognition by the Pope in the 9th century marked their allegiance to the Roman rather than the Byzantine Church. Grgur (Gregory) of Nin, a Slav bishop, tried to establish a Croatian national church, championing the use of an indigenous Croatian alphabet known as Glagolitic and the performance of Mass in the vernacular. However, his attempts were defeated by the Latin clergy.

Coveted by Hungary and Venice

The Pacta Conventa in 1102 confirmed Hungarian control over most of Croatia, although the Croats were allowed a degree of autonomy and their own representative *(ban)* and parliament *(sabor)*. The Hungarian involvement in Croatia continued for three centuries, during which they faced persistent threats from the Ottoman Empire to the east. The fear of the Islamic hordes underpinned the way Budapest viewed Croatia. Across the country's rugged interior a series of fortifications *(krajina)* were spread out as a bulwark against the Ottomans, a barrier that was ultimately successful, but often teetered on the verge of being overrun.

As Hungary secured much of inland Croatia, the Venetians moved in to snatch large swathes of coastline, over which they took control in 1420. Dubrovnik was one of the few places to retain its independence. The Venetians, like the Romans centuries earlier, brought in their own architectural ideas and town plans, leaving an indelible impression on the Croatian coast that lingers to this day in fortified towns, fine buildings and elegant church bell-towers. The Venetian hold was always tenuous, based more on securing trade routes than acquiring and governing territory, and they faced persistent threats not only from the Ottomans but also from pirates such as the infamous marauders of Senj.

Josip Jelačić enters Zagreb as ban

The Fall of the Divine Republic

As the 18th century came to a close the French, under Napoleon, finally triggered the end of the Venetian Republic in 1797. Among the booty they collected were the Venetian possessions along the Croatian coast. The history of Napoleon's 'Illyrian Provinces' was to be short-lived after the French defeat at the hands of Russia in the winter of 1812–13. The Austro-Hungarians were on hand to pick up the pieces and the Treaty of Vienna confirmed their gains in 1815.

Despite, or perhaps because of spending centuries as the subjects of various powers, Croatian identity and patriotism started to reassert itself in the first half of the 19th century, with the result that Josip Jelačić, a popular army officer from the Vojna Krajina, became *ban* (governor) of Croatia, though he was careful to pledge loyalty to the Habsburg Empire. This drive for recognition manifested itself most strongly in the cultural and linguistic fields, and it came at a time of similar Serb and Slovene risings in what evolved into a pan-Slavism movement.

World Wars I and II

The dissolution of the Austro Hungarian Empire that was precipitated by World War I presented an ideal opportunity for this pan-Slavism to become something more solid, with the formation of the Kingdom of the Serbs, Croats and Slovenes in 1918 (known as Yugoslavia after 1930). Despite high hopes and official talk of unity, many Croats were disappointed to find that instead of the loose federalism they had anticipated much of the real power shifted to Belgrade.

When Germany swept into Croatia in April 1939 extremist members of the Ustaše Party, under Ante Pavelić, seized the opportunity and collaborated in the setting up of a Nazi puppet state. The Nazis brought out the worst in some Croats, and Pavelić and his cronies established a concentration camp at Jasenovac where Serbs, Jews and other 'undesirables' were murdered. This sorry chapter in Croatia's history ended in 1945 with Tito's communist partisans taking control of Yugoslavia and massacring thousands of Ustae forces and collaborators.

Croatia under Tito

Tito (born Josip Broz, 1892–1980), himself a Croat, kept a tight rein over Yugoslavia during his four decades as president and Communist Party leader. Croatian nationalism was suppressed, as were nationalist sentiments in Bosnia, Serbia and Kosovo, though they still simmered below the surface. Economic resentment grew in Croatia from the 1960s when mass tourism started bringing in substantial amounts of hard currency, which was often siphoned away from the coast to swell central government coffers in Belgrade.

The disenchantment helped to fuel desires for greater self-government, which manifested itself in the Croatian Spring. This involved reform-minded politicians and intellectuals, some of whom called for Croatian to be recognised as a separate language from Serbian. The Croatian League of Communists was split between those who wanted to keep the status quo and those looking for greater autonomy, a tension that was expressed in student riots in the early 1970s. Seeing the unity of Yugoslavia threatened, Tito moved in to clamp down on the Croatian Spring, with sackings and forced resignations in December 1971.

Tito as a young partisan during World War II

Ethnic Rivalries and the Descent to War

While Tito had been largely successful in suppressing the worst of the ethnic rivalries within Yugoslavia, he had been less successful in grooming an heir and his death in 1980 created a power vacuum and a sense of instability that ultimately paved the way for the bloody Balkan wars of the 1990s. In the absence of Tito the Yugoslav presidency was left to a rotating collective, representing the republics.

Slovenia escapes

Slovenia declared independence from Yugoslavia on the same day as Croatia – 25 June 1991. However, with far fewer ethnic Serbs among its population and with no history of ethnic cleansing it did not provoke the savage reaction from Serbia that Croatia drew. After a brief skirmish with the Slovenes, the Yugoslav Army evacuated Slovenia with barely a murmur.

Amid political wrangling and machinations the then little-known Serbian politician Slobodan Milošević emerged to assert Serbian nationalism and endorse the view that Belgrade was not interested in letting the various parts of Yugoslavia enjoy an amicable divorce. As moves towards independence took hold in Slovenia and Croatia, many Serbs, including Milošević, realised dissolution was inevitable and instigated a plan that involved setting up a 'Greater Serbia' by swallowing large sections of the other parts of Yugoslavia.

Tensions finally reached a head in June 1991 when Slovenia and Croatia declared their independence. An ex-Yugoslav general, Franjo Tudjman, was at the helm of a new Croatian nation, which was not officially recognised by the United Nations and which faced the immediate danger of the Serbs within its borders combining with the powerful Yugoslav Army to cut off parts of its territory and claim them for 'Greater Serbia'.

The Homeland War

From June 1991 onwards the fighting escalated rapidly as the rebel Serbs and the Yugoslav National Army (the JNA) used their military superiority against the poorly armed Croatian police and guard units to 'ethnically cleanse' swathes of Croatia. Milošević gambled on a quick victory before the international community became involved, but the rapid Serb successes in central Croatia were halted in Slavonia by the defiant stand of the people of the eastern city of Vukovar. This city stood on the border with Serbia and bore the brunt of heavy shelling and air raids as it became cut off and a siege of medieval ferocity ensued. Vukovar's resistance was echoed in the south by Dubrovnik, which was also besieged. Both cities became patriotic symbols of Croatian resistance.

Although Vukovar did eventually fall and Serbian forces committed further atrocities to those that had already scarred their military advances around the country, Zagreb was never threatened. Serb military progress soon slowed as the Croats managed to gather hardware and personnel together for a more organised defence. In the spring of 1992, soon after

The Siege of Dubrovnik

The Siege of Dubrovnik was only the most publicised of a plethora of attacks from the Yugoslav Army, but it was the one that made headline news around the world. The city had no particular strategic value nor any real Serb claim of ownership (the Serb population was around 7 percent), but it was surrounded by a naval blockade and shelled from the surrounding hills for seven months, its 50,000 inhabitants trapped behind the medieval city walls. Electricity and communications were cut and the citizens found themselves sheltering in candlelit basements; even the yachts in the harbour were blown up. By the end of the siege more than 500 historic buildings had been damaged and 43 citizens killed.

Germany had unilaterally recognised Croatian independence, UN units were deployed as a buffer between the two sides following international negotiations.

The peace deal froze the battle lines and promised to return territory to the Croatians, but the vague timescale did not satisfy Tudjman. His government continued to acquire military equipment in a period when the rebel Serbs had lost the backing of the Yugoslav Army. In 1995 the Croatian 'Flash' (May) and 'Storm' (August) offensives may have incited the ire of the UN, but the Croats rapidly

Dubrovnik under siege in 1991

regained much rebel Serb territory. In 1998, as part of the Erdut agreement, the last tracts of Slavonia, including devastated Vukovar, were handed back to Croatia and the Homeland War was at an end.

With the establishment of the International War Crimes Tribunal for the former Yugoslavia at the Hague, various perpetrators of atrocities have gradually been brought to trial, though the prime culprits, Tudjman and Milošević, both died before being sentenced. The accused also include some of the Croatian officers active in Operation Storm. Charges of war crimes against Croatian forces provoked fury among many Croats, but the country has made steps to cooperate with the tribunal, such as the arrest of General Ante Gotovina in Spain in 2005.

Croatia Today

As one of Europe's newest nations Croatia has quickly established itself on the world stage, not least in sport. The national football team came third in the 1998 World Cup in France, Goran Ivanišević became the first wildcard to win Wimbledon in 2001 and the national tennis team won the Davis Cup in 2005. In 2002 Janica Kostelić won Croatia's first three Olympic gold medals and a silver in the Winter Olympics in Salt Lake City.

Croatia's emergence on the political and economic stage has been much slower, in part because in the early years the right-wing policies and abrasive style of President Franjo Tudjman marred the country's image abroad. Since his death in 1999, Croatia has been welcomed back into the international community and foreign investment has grown. The new government demonstrated its determination to enhance Croatia's profile by its improved cooperation with the War Crimes Tribunal at the Hague.

As the images of the Homeland War fade tourists are again flocking to Croatia, especially along the Adriatic coast where the hotels have been refurbished and in some cases equipped with luxurious extras, such as 'wellness centres', and the marinas are teeming with yachts.

Ivanišević winning Wimbledon

Historical Landmarks

30,000BC 'Krapina Man' evidence of prehistoric settlement in Croatia.

1000BC Illyrian tribes begin living in the region.

229BC–AD600 Roman then Byzantine empires hold sway.

600–700 Arrival of Slavic tribes from north of the Danube.

925 King Tomislav becomes the first king of an independent Croatia.

1102 Hungarian control over Croatia formalised by the Pacta Conventa.

1420s Venetian Republic occupies much of the Croatian coast.

1797 Venetian Republic collapses to Napoleon.

1918 Kingdom of Serbs, Croats and Slovenes proclaimed.

1929 Fascist Ustaše set-up under Ante Pavelić.

1939 German troops invade and Ustaše collaborates in establishing the Independent State of Croatia (NDH).

May 1945 Tito's Partisans enter Zagreb, marking the start of Communist rule. Tito is declared prime minister of the new Yugoslav Federal Republic.

1953 Tito becomes president.

1960s Croatian Spring marks a desire for independence.

1980 Death of Tito leaves power vacuum.

1990 Moves towards Croatian independence led by Franjo Tudjman.

25 June 1991 Declaration of independence; Croatian Serbs revolt with the help of Serbia and the backing of the powerful Yugoslav military. The Homeland War breaks out.

18 November 1991 Fall of Vukovar marks nadir of the war for Croatia.

January 1992 United Nations brokers a cease-fire.

1995 Croatian 'Flash' (May) and 'Storm' (August) offensives regain much of rebel Serb territory.

1998 Last occupied areas returned to Croatia through the UN.

10 December 1999 Death of President Tudjman.

January 2000 Fall of ruling HDZ and the rise of more liberal government.

2003 Croatia applies to join the European Union (EU).

2005 The arrest of alleged war criminal Ante Gotovina signals the opening of serious negotiations for EU membership.

May 2007 Trial of Ante Gotovina begins in the Hague.

WHERE TO GO

Most of Croatia's tourist industry is concentrated on the Adriatic coast, in Dalmatia and the Istrian peninsula, including the numerous islands. International airports serving the coast include Dubrovnik, Split, Zadar, Rijeka and Pula. The main coastal road is the Jadranska Magistrala (Adriatic Highway), running from Rijeka to Dubrovnik, parts of which are dual-carriageway. Island-hopping is a great way to experience coastal Croatia; the main ferry company is Jadrolinija, <www.jadrolinija.hr>.

Inland Croatia also has plenty to interest visitors, including the lively capital of Zagreb, impressive mountain scenery, castles, spas and the outstanding Plitvice Lakes National Park. From Zagreb the *autocesta* (motorway) runs east to Slavonia. The capital is also linked to Rijeka in the west by a new motorway, and another to Split in the south opened in 2005.

ZAGREB

Zagreb may never have been intended as a national capital, but since the Declaration of Independence in 1991 it has taken to its new role with a relish. Its centre has been smartened up, new shops have flourished and there has been a marked improvement in its hotels and restaurants. Gone are the old trappings of communism – Marx is out, mobile phones in.

A plethora of museums, a charming old quarter, a number of leafy parks and a lively nightlife make Zagreb an ideal city-break destination. Many people heading for the coast tend to bypass the capital and in doing so miss out on this compact, lively metropolis whose younger residents, many of them students, give it a buzz that is particularly evident in its myriad cafés on a balmy evening.

Zagreb Card

The Zagreb Card represents good value if you plan to spend some time in the city. It is valid for three days. Holders are entitled to a 50 percent reduction in admission charges to most galleries and museums and free public transport, as well as a range of theatre, restaurant and nightclub discounts. The card is available from the tourist information office on Trg Bana Josip Jelačića, or see <www.zagrebcard.fivestars.hr>.

The city is popular with business people, too, and getting a good-value room can be a problem when one of the many conferences and business events is taking place, so it is advisable to book well ahead.

Donji Grad

Spreading north of Glavni Kolodvor, the central railway station, is Donji Grad (the Lower Town). Standing proud in Trg Kralja Tomislava, the square opposite the station, is the equestrian **statue of King Tomislav**, the first of the Croatian kings, his commanding figure a meeting point for Zagreb's younger citizens, as well as a symbol of the city.

A short stroll away is the **Hotel Regent Esplanade**, a grand dame built in 1925 that was designed to accommodate passengers passing through Zagreb on the Orient Express. A substantial renovation has left the core of the ornate old building intact, including the art deco lobby with its display of clocks telling the time in various cities around the world. The hotel has a pavement café and a casino where at night many of Zagreb's movers and shakers can be seen gambling away their *kuna*. There is also a health club offering beauty treatments, a sauna and a gym.

Stretching north of the central railway station is a string of neatly tended squares, often filled with students reclining on benches and older citizens idling by the fountains. Trg Kralja Tomislava is home to the **Art Pavilion** (Umjetnički Paviljon;

open Mon–Sat 11am–7pm, Sun 10am–1pm; admission fee), an art nouveau building housing exhibitions and a restaurant.

The next park north is Strossmayer Trg, containing the **Strossmayer Gallery** (Strossmayerova Galerija; open Tues 10am–1pm and 5–7pm, Wed–Sun 10am–1pm; admission fee). It was commissioned by the eponymous Slavonian bishop in the 19th century and has a collection of works by Italian masters including Tintoretto and Veronese, dating from the 14th to 18th centuries. Look out also for the Baška Tablet, said to be the oldest example of Croatian Glagolitic script, brought here from its original home on the Kvarner Gulf island of Krk.

A few blocks west, in Trg Maršala Tita, is the **Arts and Crafts Museum** (Muzej za Umjetnost i Obrt; open Tues–Sat 10am–7pm, Sun 10am–2pm; admission fee; <www.muo.hr>), designed by the Austrian architect Hermann Bollé, whose name pops up all over the city, including the Mirogoj Cemetery *(see*

The Art Pavilion in spring

page 33). The eclectic collection includes ceramics and furniture, clocks, silverware, glass and religious art.

Diagonally opposite the museum, facing Rooseveltov Trg, is Zagreb's most impressive museum: the **Mimara** (Muzej Mimara; open Tues–Wed, Fri–Sat 10am–5pm, Thur 10am–7pm, Sun 10am–2pm; admission fee), housed in an old grammar school. The artists represented include Raphael, Caravaggio, Rembrandt, Rubens, Van Dyck, Velasquez, Gainsborough, Turner, Delacroix, Renoir, Manet and Degas. There have been persistent mutterings from certain sections of the art world about the dubious authenticity of some of the work, but if you take it on face value the 4,000-strong collection is impressive. The contents were donated to the city by Dalmatian collector Ante Topić Mimara and also include archaeological finds from around the Mediterranean. The sculpture collection includes works by Rodin, Robbia and Verocchio.

Trg Bana Josip Jelačića sets the pace of the city

Trg Bana Josip Jelačića

The epicentre of Zagreb life, **Trg Bana Josip Jelačića**, is surrounded by grand 19th-century buildings. The statue of the viceroy, Ban Josip Jelačić, erected in 1866 and banished by Tito in 1945, has been returned to its prominent position at the heart of this plaza. Today, the square is the best place to take the pulse of the city,

Angels on Zagreb Cathedral

so pull up a chair, order a coffee and absorb a scene as far removed as possible from any lingering images that you may have of a former communist city. Slick new trams ease past the trundling models of the communist era, while mobile-phone-carrying executives vie for space with Zagreb's bright young things, who would not be seen dead walking across the square in anything other than the latest designer fashion.

Kaptol

The Kaptol district breaks away uphill from Trg Bana Josip Jelačića. Without doubt, the highlight here is the neo-Gothic **Zagreb Cathedral** (opening times vary; free) with its twin bell-towers, designed by Hermann Bollé. A religious building has stood on the site since the reign of the Croatian kings in the 10th century and it is still a place of devotion for many local residents. Notable features include a series of 13th-century frescoes that have survived the cathedral's numerous traumas, including a devastating earthquake in the 19th century. The cathedral is also the last resting place of the controversial Croatian clergyman Archbishop Stepinac (d.1960), who was accused of colluding with the Nazi puppet regime during World War II, but is considered a martyr by many Croats. Look out for Ivan Meštrović's relief of Christ with Stepinac. Outside the cathedral is a striking work by the Austrian artist Anton Fernkorn (1813–78), a gleaming gold Madonna surrounded by angels.

Situated a short walk west from the cathedral is **Dolac Market**. This atmospheric spot is an antidote to Zagreb's new air-conditioned malls and designer boutiques. Bargain-hunting locals can be seen haggling over the fresh fruit, flowers and vegetables in a scene virtually unchanged since communist times. A sprinkling of modest bars and restaurants overlook the small market square, providing a good

Fresh produce in Dolac Market

view of the action. For those who are planning on catching a train from Zagreb to Budapest, Vienna or to the Croatian coastline, the market is a good place to stock up on provisions.

Gornji Grad

The oldest part of the city is the Gornji Grad (Upper Town), which still retains some of its historical charm. You can reach it by walking up from the cathedral, but it is more fun to take the funicular from Donji Grad. At the top is the **Lotršćak Tower** (Kula Lotršćak; open Tues–Sun 11am–7pm; admission fee), where an art gallery with a modest array of paintings for sale is a prelude to the main attraction – a sweeping view of the city from the observation level.

Below the tower, **Strossmayer Parade** (Strossmayerovo Šetalište) offers similarly fine views of the city spreading across the plain, with its main buildings, including the cathedral, clearly visible. The most intriguing bench from which to savour the vista is the work of modern artist Ivan Kožari, with the bronze figure of the writer Antun Gustav Matoš awaiting someone to share the view with him.

The easy way to the Upper Town is to take the funicular

A short walk north brings you to **St Mark's Church** (opening times vary; free), which is currently undergoing a major renovation. This striking church features a multi-coloured 19th-century roof, upon which the Croatian coat of arms is clearly visible. The church itself dates back to the 13th century, though there have been many major renovations over the centuries. Inside are several works by Ivan Meštrović, including a sinewy depiction of Christ on the cross in typically challenging Meštrović style.

Fans of the 20th-century cult Croatian sculptor will not want to miss the **Meštrović Atelier** (open Tues–Fri 10am–6pm, Sat–Sun 10am–2pm; admission fee), just north of St Mark's. Meštrović lived here from 1924 to 1942 and the displays of his original sketches and plans illuminate many of the works that can be seen around Zagreb, including the *Crucifixion* in St Mark's Church and the statue of Grgur of Nin, outside

Diocletian's Palace in Split, with a replica in Varaždin.

Located further north, the **Museum of Zagreb** (Muzej Grada Zagreba; open Tues–Fri 10am–6pm, Sat–Sun 10am–1pm; admission fee) features, among other displays, scale models that help visitors to understand the different phases of the city from medieval times to the modern day. There is also a section on the Homeland War, covering the Serb attacks on the fledgling capital, including the Yugoslav Air Force's audacious attempt to assassinate President Tudjman in his Presidential Palace in Zagreb.

Pavement cafés abound

In the shadow of the Gornji Grad is **Tkalčićeva**. This cobbled thoroughfare is lined with pavement cafés and on busy nights it is packed with locals out to see and be seen. There are so many cafés to choose from the best option is to stroll along its length a couple of times before you settle down and order your coffee or an Ožujsko, the excellent locally brewed lager.

Parks and Gardens

Zagreb's green spaces provide a welcome escape from the bustle of city life on a hot day. Within walking distance of the centre are the **Botanical Gardens** (Botanički Vrt; open daily 9am–sunset; free), established at the end of the 19th century. Around 10,000 species are packed into small confines, surrounded by paths and benches, and one of the pools is home to carp and a colony of terrapins. Not many tourists yet know about this garden, which makes it particularly appealing.

Maksimir Park is only a short tram ride 3km (1¾ miles) east of the city centre and spreads out across 128 hectares (316 acres). Both the national football team and local side Dinamo Zagreb (whose name was changed during the Tudjman years to Croatia Zagreb) play their home games at the crumbling sports stadium facing the park. The atmosphere during games can be rowdy, but there is no better venue to see both Croatian patriotism and the local citizens' love of Zagreb expressed so vehemently. Within the park boundaries are **Zagreb Zoo** (June–Sept 9am–8pm, Oct–May 9am–5pm; admission fee), a boating lake and walkways, as well as plenty of shady trees.

Mirogoj Cemetery

When President Tudjman was laid to rest in December 1999 there was only one place suitable for the leader who had brought Croatia through its traumatic divorce from Yugoslavia in a blaze of showy glory. The Mirogoj Cemetery (free) is the place to be if you are dead in Zagreb. Here, in one of Europe's grandest graveyards, the city's richest residents and luminaries vie for space.

A local joke makes fun of the fact that many of the deceased inhabitants of Mirogoj have far more impressive abodes than the living citizens of the city, and there is more than a little truth to this. The cemetery was built in 1876, the majority of it the work of Herman Bollé, whose extravagant tastes and designs are evident both here and elsewhere in the city. The entrance is particularly striking: an elegant neo-classical façade draped in ivy with a colonnade and a row of four lime green cupolas topped off with one large central dome.

It is worth spending some time admiring the sculptures and grand tombs that grace the interior. Look out too for the memorial to the victims of the Homeland War, with a monument inscribed with the names of 13,500 dead, situated just outside the main gate.

There are regular buses from the cathedral to Mirogoj Cemetery.

Lake Jarun is also only a short tram ride from the city centre, 4km (2½ miles) to the southwest. This park rose to prominence when Zagreb hosted the World Student Games in 1987 and its artificial lake was the scene of the rowing events. The action is of a more nefarious kind on steamy summer weekend evenings, when local teenagers grab their cheap bottles of booze and head down here to frolic. For more discerning visitors there are cafés, restaurants and bars that are open day and night in summer. Lake Jarun is also good for bracing strolls in winter, as are the banks of the River Sava, recently enlivened by public sculptures.

INLAND CROATIA

North of Zagreb

Varaždin is the only city in the **Zagorje** region, which extends north of Zagreb towards Hungary and Slovenia. The Zagorje is a hilly green playground for the citizens of Zagreb, who come to visit the chocolate-box castles, relax in the spas and sample the local food and drink. A good

Baroque elegance in Varaždin

sweep of the Zagorje can be covered in a long day trip from Zagreb, but to get a real feel for this rewarding region it is worth basing yourself in Varaždin for a few days.

Varaždin's old town is being smartened up by the ambitious council and there are also plans to have the city's main tourist attraction, **Stari Grad Fortress** (open high season Tues–Sun 10am–6pm; low season Tues–Fri 10am–3pm, Sat–Sun 10am–1pm; admission fee), put on UNESCO's World Heritage list. The fortifications date back to the 16th century when the castle was built as part of an attempt by the Austrian-Hungarians to fend off the attentions of the Ottoman Empire. When the threat of Ottoman invasion ceased, the local Erdödy family bought the fortress and transformed it into a grand home. Varaždin's City Museum is housed in the castle and a range of temporary exhibitions are held in the basement.

Trakošćan Castle

Stari Grad Fortress is one of a string of castles that are spread out over the Zagorje, set amid the rolling hills and forests that characterise the landscape. **Trakošćan Castle** (open Apr–Sept 9am–6pm, Oct–Mar 9am–3pm; admission fee; <www.mdc.hr/trakoscan>), less than an hour's drive west of Varaždin, and another popular excursion from the capital, is one of the most appealing. A castle has stood on the site since the 16th century, but the one that is open to the public today is largely the result of a rather fanciful 19th-century remoulding. The castle is worth a few hours' exploration, as are the surrounding grounds where a small lake has a path running around its shores and a café by the water's edge.

The Zagorje gained a reputation as a spa retreat in the 19th century when visitors from Austria would come to take the waters. Of the spas left today, **Krapinske Toplice** (admission fee) is one of the best. There are number of pools of varying temperature, from lukewarm to steaming hot, where you can join in the relaxed fun.

Plitvice Lakes

The **Plitvice Lakes National Park** (Plitvička Jezera; admission fee; <www.np-plitvicka-jezera.hr>), 110km (68 miles) south of Zagreb on the old road to Split, is one of Croatia's top attractions, and justifiably so. The park was added to UNESCO's World Heritage list in 1979, and although it suffered during the 1990s from Serb occupation, it is now back in business.

Whatever the season, the beauty of Plitvice is immediately evident. The fresh, clear waters rush through a network of 16 lakes and tumble down waterfalls stretching for some 8km (5 miles). You can visit the lakes on a day trip from Zagreb or from the southern cities and resorts, but it is best to spend a night at one of the state-owned hotels inside the park boundaries. Wildlife within the park includes otter and deer, wild boar and even bears, not to mention a wide variety of fish and birds.

Croatia's Plitvice Lakes are among Europe's top natural attractions

Getting around Plitvice could not be easier, as the trails and wooden walkways are connected by boats and tourist trains. Hopping on and off the boats and traversing the wooden walkways as the spray of the waterfalls mists all around is part of the fun.

In high season don't be deterred by the crowds: set off early in the morning and head south to Lake Proščansko, which is usually quiet and peaceful all year round. Often the best plan is to divide your visit into at least two adventures: one to the remote upper lakes and another to the more popular lower lakes, avoiding the temptation to cover everything too quickly. Swimming in the lakes is prohibited.

Slavonia

The often neglected eastern region of Slavonia has plenty to offer, not least the fact that even at the height of summer it is never overrun with tourists. It lies just a 3-hour drive east along the *autocesta* (motorway) from Zagreb. The last part of occupied Slavonia was only handed back to Croatia in 1998.

The city of Osijek is a good base, but 35km (22 miles) along the trunk road from the *autocesta* to Osijek it is worth stopping off at the small town of **Đakovo** to visit its stunning cathedral whose lofty twin towers can be seen from afar. The neo-Gothic cathedral, built between 1862 and 1882, was commissioned by the legendary Croatian clergyman Bishop Strossmayer. A sculpture of Strossmayer sits gazing back towards the monumental building from across the road.

Osijek was subject to savage Serb attacks during the Homeland War, but today the city is regaining its verve, with cafés reopening along the River Drava and the local student population providing the new blood needed to get it back on its feet. The core of the city is blessed with some impressive

Jasenovac Camp

Jasenovac is a name that stains the 20th-century history of Croatia and that continues to simmer below the surface today. The World War II concentration camp that was built in the woods southwest of Zagreb on the way to Slavonia saw thousands of Serbs, Jews and other 'undesirables' put to death amid savage conditions. Much debate in the 1970s and 1980s focused on how many hundreds of thousands were killed here, but these squabbles are just a background to the brute fact of the camp's existence. Jasenovac was occupied by Serbian forces during the Homeland War and many of the surviving objects were removed. A Memorial Museum (open Mon–Fri 9am–5pm, Sat–Sun 10am–4pm; free) opened on this site in 2006.

Osijek's cathedral, one of many fine cathedrals in eastern Croatia

architecture, most notably on Europska Avenija which has a collage of art nouveau buildings. The massive Cathedral of St Peter and St Paul, built in neo-Gothic style at the end of the 19th century, was commissioned by Bishop Strossmayer.

A 10-minute stroll from Europska is **Tvrđa**. This old quarter has been neglected for decades and the Serbs shelled it heavily in the early 1990s, but recent efforts to shore up the roofs have revived the area. The Catholic Church, both in Croatia and overseas, has also spent much time and money resurrecting the exteriors and interiors of the many churches housed within the old walls. Tvrđa was originally built by the Habsburgs as a bulwark against the Ottoman Empire and its rich history is now starting to be unearthed.

Vukovar is a name that conjures up a whole range of emotions in any Croat. It enjoys a scenic position on the banks of the River Danube, and was once a pleasant baroque town inhabited by a mix of Croats, Serbs, Bosnians, Germans and Slovaks among others. Tragically for Vukovar it also lay on the eastern edge of the new Republic of Croatia and in 1991 the political leaders in Belgrade conspired with local Serbs to 'ethnically cleanse' the town.

With the full might of the Yugoslav army and air force, backed by Serbian volunteers, stacked up against it, few gave the hastily assembled Vukovar defence forces any chance of holding out for more than a few days. And yet from May to November 1991 Vukovar stood firm as the Serbs pummelled the town with up to 10,000 shells a day. Residents cowered in their cellars without electricity and scarce supplies of food and water, their only escape route being the mined cornfields on the town's perimeter. When the Serbs took the devastated town they committed their final horror by staying true to their war cry: 'There will be meat when we take Vukovar, for we'll slaughter the Croats.' They snatched 200 Croats from under the noses of the Red Cross at the local hospital and massacred them in a field near the town where a memorial now stands.

Visiting Vukovar today gives a real sense of what happened to Croatia during the war – something that is not easy to appreciate in the glossy coastal resorts. Any doubts about whether it is distasteful to visit the town are soon dispelled by the remaining residents. They are only too happy to see outsiders who take an interest in the suffering that they felt was ignored by the rest of Europe. Tourism is crucial to the recovery of Vukovar and, on a larger scale, to Slavonia.

Commemorating Vukovar's dead

Early morning view of Rovinj, one of the prettiest towns in Istria

ISTRIA

Istria, the triangular-shaped peninsula that extends into the Adriatic in the extreme north of the Croatian seaboard, is the country's most popular tourist destination. Since the 1960s visitors have been pouring into the purpose-built resorts in and around Rovinj, Vrsar, Umag, Novigrad and the busiest of them all, Poreč. The Homeland War did not directly affect Istria, and tourism is back on track with refurbished hotels and new developments. These include the *Agroturizam* programme, which has transformed old farmhouses into restaurants and small hotels.

Istria's only city is Pula, whose fine amphitheatre is a reminder of the time when the Romans held sway over the peninsula. Their empire left numerous traces in Croatia and the central cores of both Pula and Poreč are still built on the original Roman plan. The Venetians, too, left their mark on

Istria, most notably in the coastal town of Rovinj and in the interior, where Venetian fortifications are the legacy of the days when pirates and Ottomans threatened the trade routes and the Istrian peninsula.

Pula

Croatia's Roman heritage is most impressive in **Pula**. The city's dramatic legacy from its days as Polensium is the **Roman Amphitheatre** (open May–Sept 8am–9pm, Oct–Apr 9am–3pm; admission fee), standing proud near the waterfront. Originally the amphitheatre would have attracted around 23,000 spectators to its bloody entertainment; today it is still pulling in the punters for rock and classical concerts. A small museum is housed in the vaults, but the main attraction is just walking around with the ghosts of the Romans in this 2,000-year-old arena.

James Joyce

James Joyce aficionados may want to follow the trail left in Pula by the great Irish writer before he flitted north to Trieste and set about finishing *A Portrait of the Artist as a Young Man* and embarking on his epic *Ulysses*. The tourist office is keen to push the minimal Joyce connection, and the local branch of the Berlitz language school where he found work in 1904 is now open as the Uliks (Ulysses) Café. Outside the café is a bronze sculpture of Joyce sitting at his favourite chair, with his trademark hat and walking stick. The sculpture was designed by local artist Mate Čvrljak and it has become almost obligatory to have your photo taken with the author.

Not that Joyce was all that enamoured with Istria. In a letter from Pula dated 1904, he described Istria as 'a long boring place wedged into the Adriatic, peopled by ignorant Slavs who wear red caps and colossal breeches'.

The Roman Amphitheatre in Pula

Finds from Polensium are displayed in the Archaeological Museum just south of the amphitheatre. Its Sculpture Garden forms a delightful venue for classical concerts in summer.

Other interesting remnants of Roman rule include the **Triumphal Arch of Sergius**, the **Temple of Augustus** and the remains of the **Roman Forum**. The tourist office offers maps detailing the most worthwhile sights of Polensium, traces of which can be found in such inauspicious places as the bus station, where the Roman walls can be seen.

Pula's **Cathedral of St Mary** is a testament to the eventual victory of Christianity over paganism. Parts of it date from the 4th century, and some of it was built from stone lifted from the Roman amphitheatre after the demise of Polensium. The cathedral has undergone numerous renovations over the years, many of which can be easily traced, such as the 4th-century rear wall, the 13th-century sacristy and the 17th-century belltower.

Vodnjan

The road north to the resorts passes through **Vodnjan**, 10km (6 miles) from Pula. This fairly nondescript inland town is known for its 'mummies' in St Blaise's Church. Some devout Croats believe that the mummies possess magical powers, but many of today's visitors just come for the ghoulish appeal of viewing the desiccated corpses of St Nikolosa Bursa, St Giovanni Olini and St Leon Bembo. Vodnjan itself is worth a wander, and there are a couple of small restaurants if you want to stay for lunch or dinner.

Rovinj

About 50km (30 miles) north along the E751 from Pula is **Rovinj,** the most attractive town on the Istrian littoral. The approach to Rovinj is spectacular, with views of the old town clustered on a hilly peninsula in a collage of orange roof tiles and cobbled streets. In summer the streets can be busy, but the big hotel developments and campsites are outside the old town so much of the historical core remains unspoilt.

Dominating Rovinj from its highest spot is the church of **St Euphemia**. This 18th-century baroque creation features Istria's tallest bell-tower, which has been used for centuries by local fishermen both for weather forecasts and as a landmark for seeking their way home. Legend has it that the body of St Euphemia arrived shrouded in mystery in her weighty sarcophagus on the Rovinj shoreline. No one could budge the bulky stone tomb until a local boy and his two cows conspired with divine intervention to spirit her to her last resting place. The sarcophagus is now inside the church.

The **Town Museum** (open June–Sept Tues–Sun 9am– noon, 7–10pm, Oct–May Tues–Sat 9am–1pm; admission fee; <www.muzej-rovinj.com>) makes a good attempt at delving into the town's history. As well as playing host to temporary exhibitions, it has a permanent collection of Istrian folk costumes and finds from local archaeological digs, as well as paintings from the 15th and 16th centuries. The highlight is Pietro Mera's *Christ Crowned with Thorns*.

For children, a good distraction outside the old town is **Rovinj Aquarium** (open Apr–Oct 9am–9pm; admission fee). The aquarium was built in 1891 and although it is not exactly state-of-the-art, it is home to a colourful collection of Istrian sealife. It has a more serious side as part of the Ruđer Bošković Centre for Maritime Research.

One of Rovinj's most appealing streets is **Grisia**, a narrow lane that sneaks

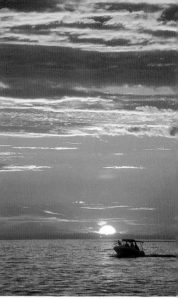

Rovinj is known for its sunsets

north from sea level up to the church of St Euphemia. Grisia is charming enough in itself, with fine views of the church unfolding as you ascend, but it is also home to Rovinj's thriving artistic community. The enlightened local authorities have encouraged painters and craftsmen to live and work along Grisia and more than a dozen small shops now have the artists' eclectic work on sale. Much of it is blatantly geared towards the tourist trade, but usually there are some interesting pieces to be found if you look carefully.

One of the great pleasures in Rovinj is doing nothing other than dipping in and out of the Adriatic Sea. As with most of Istria there are no real beaches as such, only a ramble of rocks around the old town peninsula, as well as concrete platforms and steps for less agile bathers. In summer the water is warm, and calm enough for families. Lining the waterfront on the southern side of the old town are cafés and restaurants where bathers can refuel.

Poreč

About 30km (20 miles) north of Rovinj is **Poreč**, the epicentre of Istria's tourist industry, with attractive Venetian-style architecture. The town buzzes in high season as British and German voices mingle among Croatian and Italian tongues along the old Roman thoroughfares. Despite throngs of holidaymakers, the old town retains its character because many of the area's hotels and campsites are located in the purpose-built resort of Zelena Laguna. In high season Poreč's waterfront is lined with bobbing tour boats, the restaurants offer tourist menus and there are myriad watersports on offer.

Istrian Wines

Wine has been popular in Istria since Roman times and the industry has enjoyed a renaissance over the last few years. Both large-scale producers and small family-run vineyards have invested in modern machinery and techniques, improving the standards of what were already fine wines.

Both red and white wines are produced on the peninsula. Look out for Muscatel and Malvazija whites and the Teran red. These wines are available in shops all over Istria, though they are expensive when bottled – which is why many locals travel out to vineyards themselves to buy in bulk. The Istria County Tourist Association has produced the Guide to the Wine Roads of Istria with a map and details of the vineyards where you can sample and buy wine. It is available from tourist offices in Istria. See also <www.istra.com/vino>.

The exquisite mosaics in the Basilica of Euphrasius in Poreč

Tourism apart, Poreč's greatest attraction is the UNESCO World Heritage listed **Basilica of Euphrasius** (open daily 7am–7pm; admission fee for bell-tower), one of the most remarkable examples of Byzantine art in the world. The scattering of buildings inside the main complex occupy the site of a 4th-century church, whose mosaics can be seen in the apse just inside the main door of today's basilica. The ebullient gold and mother-of-pearl studded scenes of the Virgin and Child, the Annunciation and Visitation are captivating, so take a seat and let them work their magic.

The remnants of Poreč's **Roman Heritage** are also worth investigating. The Romans made Poreč what it is today with their sturdy town plan, and its main thoroughfares are still evident, though these days they are lined with shops, cafés and restaurants. Follow Decumanus down from Zagrebačka to trace the heart of Roman Poreč, a walk culminating at what is left of the Forum. Look out for the

Sailing to the Brijuni Islands

Romanesque House, built many centuries after the Romans left Istria and now housing an art gallery.

Other Coastal Resorts

Development is continuing along the coast. Between Rovinj and Poreč is **Vrsar**, a quieter resort than Poreč. South of town is **Koversada**, one of the world's largest naturist resorts.

To the north of Poreč towards the Slovenian border are the resorts of **Umag** and **Novigrad**. Novigrad is the more attractive of the two – a sort of mini-Rovinj complete with a bell-tower overlooking a town that curls around a peninsula – though there are some unattractive hotel developments dating from the communist era. It also has some good fish restaurants. Umag is appealing in a less ostentatious way, and has its moment in the spotlight every July when the Croatian Tennis Open brings in big international names, as well as local stars.

On Istria's quieter east coast, hillside **Labin** is the largest and most interesting settlement. Its neighbour, **Rabac**, offers excellent beaches and lively nightlife.

Boat Trips from the Coastal Resorts

Between May and October there are regular boat excursions from all the Istrian resorts. The trips, either half- or full-day, often include lunch and can be booked at hotels or at the boats themselves on the previous evening, or even, subject to availability, on the day. One of the most popular excursions is to the **Brijuni Islands**, <www.brijuni.hr>, a string of verdant islands that were given national park status in 1983. Public access is only allowed on two of them, Veli Brijun and Mali Brijun, and even then visitors either have to be staying at one of the hotels on Veli Brijun or be on one of the organised tours.

The islands were once a retreat for Tito, who spent much of his time entertaining world dignitaries here. These guests are said to have brought many of the animals at Brijuni Zoo as gifts for the communist leader.

Limski Zaljev (Lim Fjord) is one of the most dramatic day trips. The steep walls of the fjord are covered with lush vegetation and were once a hideaway for pirates. Lunch in one of the waterside restaurants is highly recommended as the mussels and oysters are superb. Visitors with their own transport can also take the old road from Rovinj to Poreč and stop off to savour some of the best seafood in Croatia.

Fishermen examine their catch at Lim Fjord

Beside the castle in the old quarter of Pazin

Istrian Interior

While the coast attracts the holidaymakers, the hinterland remains mostly unexplored. The rolling green landscape of scenic hill towns and winding roads is blessed with many fine wines, truffles to match the best Italy and France have to offer and rustic places to savour the food and drink of the region. It is being dubbed the 'New Tuscany' and is where Agroturizam is opening up traditional farmhouses as restaurants and guesthouses *(see page 105)*.

A 35-km (22-mile) drive east of Poreč is Istria's rather unlikely regional capital, **Pazin**, which is a good base for exploring the interior, although it is by no means as attractive as many of the smaller hill towns. The main attractions are the castle (open May–Oct Tues–Sun 10am–6pm; Nov–Apr Tues–Thur 10am–3pm, Fri noon–5pm, Sat and Sun 11am–5pm; admission fee) and the plunging limestone gorge that descends more than 100m (328ft) below the town centre. This vertiginous drop was said to have been the inspiration for Jules Verne when he propelled the eponymous protagonist of his novel *Matthias Sandorf* over the abyss. Some say the spectacular chasm may also have prompted Dante to pen his *Inferno*.

The archetypal Istrian hill town is **Motovun**, situated 20km (12 miles) northeast of Poreč. Motovun has it all: the vineyards on the approach through the valley of the Mirna River and the winding road up the green slopes to an orange-roofed old town that harbours Roman and Venetian remnants. There are cosy cafés and small restaurants where the local cuisine can be sampled. The best way to get acquainted with Motovun is to take to its Venetian walls and wander around the old stone defences, surveying the tiled rooftops on one side and the rolling countryside on the other. Look out for the small village of Livade just below Motovun, where the truffle company Zigante Tartufi is based.

Buzet is also renowned for its high quality truffles. Every year in September there is a Truffle Festival and in season the men and their dogs can be seen heading out into the forests hunting for the pungent delicacy. Restaurants all over Istria serve truffles with pasta as well as steak with black truffle sauce. Those who are self-catering may like to buy truffle products at the Zigante Tartufi outlets in Pula, Buzet, Livade and Buje.

Grožnjan, to the west of Motovun, is a shining example of what can be done with a crumbling old town by forward thinking local authorities. Grožnjan was slowly dying until a flurry of artists and craftsmen were

A woodworker in Grožnjan

tempted into its narrow cobbled streets by the promise of free or low rents and refurbished houses. Today, the art scene flourishes with dozens of workshops. An international summer college for young musicians is based in Grožnjan, and this hilly outcrop is often bathed in the sounds of classical music. The town is pedestrianised, making it ideal for an unhurried morning or afternoon browsing through the workshops.

KVARNER GULF

The Kvarner Gulf is the wide island-studded basin that separates the Istrian peninsula in the north from the Dalmatian regions in the south. In many ways it offers the best of both areas with well-developed resort facilities along with rustic towns to explore. Transport links are good, too: a new motorway stretches from Zagreb to Rijeka (toll fee), and there are road links to Dalmatia and Istria, as well as ferry services to Dalmatia and train links from Zagreb to Rijeka.

The most interesting areas of the Kvarner Gulf are the coastal towns and resorts and the litter of islands, whereas much of the hinterland is an unforgiving and undeveloped wildscape. The harsh face of the interior is omnipresent with the voluminous wall of the Velebit range hanging over the gulf and bringing in summer thunderstorms and the bitter *bura* wind. The Velebit Mountains also present walkers and mountaineers with both adventure and spectacular views over the Kvarner Gulf.

Rijeka

Situated on the Kvarner Gulf's northern shore, **Rijeka** is the only city in the region and an important transport hub, with a major ferry terminal and an airport on the nearby

View over the Kvarner Gulf

island of Krk. The town experienced a golden age as a thriving Adriatic port under the Habsburg Empire. From the 19th century trains linked it to Vienna and Budapest. Today this industrial metropolis is making a concerted effort to tempt tourists to stay for a day or two rather than breeze through in search of the next ferry or bus. There is a new pedestrian bridge across the Mrtvi Canal and street art is brightening up the public spaces.

Rijeka's main thoroughfare is the elegant Korzo, which cuts through the heart of the city and is home to many of its best shops, cafés and most impressive buildings. To get a feel for the city, idle for a while at a café and survey the scene. Then venture into **Stari Grad** (the Old Town) through the medieval City Tower and you'll come upon another world, far removed from the 19th-century order outside. This scruffy historic quarter has a Roman Arch, as well as the church of **St Vitus**, dedicated to the city's patron saint. Parts of the church date from the 17th century and were modelled on Santa Maria della Salute Basilica in Venice. A local legend has it that one unfortunate vandal paid for his desecration of the church by being swallowed whole by the ground, never to be seen again.

For a sweeping view of the city take a bus up the steep hill to the 13th-century castle at **Trsat**, or tackle the 561 steps. This may not be one of Europe's most attractive castles, but the views are good and in summer there are classical concerts in the grounds and a pleasant open-air café. Nearby, the church of **Our Lady of Trsat** is a place of pilgrimage, particularly for women whose messages of thanks and pleas for help line the interior. Legend has it that this church was where the House of Mary and Joseph came to rest in the 13th century after fleeing Nazareth en route to Italy. It is said to have remained on the site where the church is today for three years before continuing its journey across the Adriatic.

The Opatija Riviera

Known as the Opatija Riviera, the eastern extremity of the Istrian peninsula, a short drive southwest of Rijeka, was a favourite playground for the 19th-century Viennese, who came here to escape the winter cold and seek cures for their various ailments. With a famously mild climate afforded by its unparalleled setting between the Adriatic and the Učka Mountains, it is easy to see its attraction.

Opatija itself is one of the few year-round coastal resorts in Croatia. The town has retained many of its

Past recreation

Opatija has an air of faded grandeur. Enjoy a Sachertorte and a Viennese-style coffee in the terrace café of the Millennium Hotel to capture the spirit of its 19th-century heyday.

Opatija's elegant 19th-century waterfront

grand 19th-century hotels, as well as the waterfront Lungomare, a promenade that is packed with bronzed bodies in summer and is still a pleasant place for strolls even in winter. The graceful waterfront gardens and elegant buildings still speak of the affluent days when Opatija became one of Europe's top tourist destinations, not least following the completion of the rail line from Vienna to Trieste in 1873.

The Lungomare connects Opatija with **Volosko** to the north and **Lovran** to the south. Sleepy Volosko makes for an enjoyable morning stroll, particularly if you reward your efforts with lunch in one of its seafood restaurants. Lovran is a mini-Opatija with some hotels and buildings that hark back to the riviera's golden age. There are good cafés and restaurants and opportunities for bathing. Lovran is also a good base if you are planning to walk in the **Učka Mountains**; information is available from the local tourist office.

Paklenica National Park

The scenery southeast of Rijeka is spectacular, with the Velebit mountain range towering above the barren coast, but there are few attractions other than the small town of **Senj**. In the 16th century Senj became infamous as the base from which the Uskoks warriors would set forth to attack shipping on the Adriatic.

Further south, the **Paklenica National Park** (admission charge; <www.paklenica.hr>) is a paradise for walkers, mountaineers and rock climbers. From the town of Starigrad a series of trails caters for all levels of agility and ability. The park is well organised and information and maps are obtainable from the national park office in Starigrad. If you are planning a long hike, basic mountain hut-style accommodation is available, but hotels (and hunting) are banned from the park. There are two main gorges: Mala Paklenica and Velika Paklenica, literally 'small' and 'big' Paklenica. The latter is the more user-friendly, with a well-marked main trail that snakes up in a 2-hour walk from the car park.

Hiking Opportunities

In addition to visiting Paklenica National Park, keen hikers may like to explore the rugged Mt Učka massif, accessible from towns along the coast between Poklon Pass in the north to Plomin Bay in the south. Facilities are not extensive, but there are a few mountain lodges and stone cottages for hikers, a restaurant at Poklon and a viewpoint tower on the peak of Vojak. For Vojak, the highest peak (1,394 metres/ 4,596ft), climb through Lovran's old town and follow the steps that lead up the hillside to the village of Liganj and on to the hamlets of Didici and Ivulici. The ascent can be managed in around four hours, but take provisions.

Family fun at Baška on the island of Krk

Kvarner Gulf Islands

The most popular of the Kvarner Gulf islands is **Krk**, particularly among Austrians, Hungarians and Germans, for whom it is an easy drive south and across the bridge (toll fee). **Krk Town** retains a semblance of its historic ambience with a solid old core and a few worthwhile churches. The nearby resort of **Baška** is the most appealing on the island, with a good 2-km (1¼-mile) long beach (a Blue Flag winner) and the brooding Velebit Mountains visible on the mainland. As well as having modern hotels and campsites, Baška has a small old quarter with good seafood restaurants and pension-style accommodation. It is essential to book ahead in high season.

Baška is famous for the 12th-century Baška Tablet (now in the Academy of Arts and Science in Zagreb), the oldest existing example of Glagolitic script, the precursor of Cyrillic and used in Croatia until well into the Middle Ages.

A small car ferry departs daily in summer from Baška

A picture-perfect ensemble of bell-towers in Rab

across the channel to the less-developed island of **Rab**, home to picture-perfect **Rab Town**. It is also possible to take a ferry from Jablanac in Northern Dalmatia across to Rab, which is worth considering if you are planning a journey along the coastline.

The island has a number of modest resorts and villages, but Rab Town is its undoubted star, with a well-preserved old quarter punctuated by church spires and cobbled streets. Swimming in the shadow of the pine trees beneath the old walls is a memorable experience. There are also regular taxi-boats serving beaches located in isolated bays around the island.

Rab Town's nightlife is the liveliest on the Kvarner Gulf, making it popular with younger travellers. But it is also popular with families and the island has an unmistakable buzz in high season.

Although you can see **Pag** from Rab, and there is a catamaran service from Rab to Novalja on Pag, getting there can often be frustrating. For those staying in Rab Town the island is best reached on an organised boat trip. Pag is famous for both its cheese *(paški sir)*, which is found on menus throughout Croatia, and also for intricate hand-made lace. Both products are made by small-scale producers and are available in the villages. **Pag Town** is the best base for exploring the island.

Of the two main islands on the western side of the Kvarner Gulf – Cres and Lošinj – Cres is the most northerly, with ferry connections from Istria, Rijeka and Krk. **Cres Town** makes a good base for travelling the length of the island. Colourful houses encircle its busy harbour from where fishermen supply the local restaurants. A highlight in the north of the island are the Griffon Vultures of Beli. These impressive creatures can be observed in their own protected sanctuary at Beli (<www.supovi.hr>).

Lošinj lies across a narrow channel to the south of Cres. The two main towns are Mali and Veli Losinj. **Mali Lošinj** is more developed and attracts those in search of louder bars and a choice of day trips. In contrast, **Veli Lošinj** has a more rustic appeal, but enough facilities to ensure an enjoyable stay. There are a number of islets dotted around Lošinj that can be explored by day, and by night Italian influenced seafood awaits at the waterfront restaurants of both towns.

Dolphins of Lošinj

The dolphins of Lošinj attracted international attention with the launch of the award winning Adriatic Dolphin Project in 1987. Covering the islands of Cres and Lošinj, the project aims to discover more about the dolphins' way of life as well as to help in their protection. It is believed that there may be as many as 150 bottlenose dolphins in the waters around the islands, something that yachtsmen can confirm, with many passing boats enjoying a very special escort.

Swimming with dolphins is prohibited, but those wanting to get involved can volunteer to become part of the project for 12 days. When the weather is suitable the time is spent out at sea recording, dating and tracking the creatures, and direct contact with them is common. In poor weather there are lectures and the chance to delve into the project's archives. For details see <www.blue-world.org>, where you can also 'adopt a dolphin'.

DALMATIA

Dalmatia is the long sinewy arm of Croatia that sweeps southeast from the Kvarner Gulf towards the border with Montenegro, hugging the Bosnian border for much of its length. Its coastline is punctuated by historic cities and towns and littered with myriad offshore islands, each with its own allure. The Homeland War hit parts of Dalmatia badly and while the images of Dubrovnik being shelled made TV news bulletins around the world *(see page 20)* it was the northern cities of Zadar and Šibenik that fared worst, as well as many smaller towns and villages.

Today much of the war damage has been repaired and you can spend a week or two in Dalmatia without noticing anything unusual, but a closer look reveals the different shades of roof tiles and hastily repaired churches that tell their own baleful stories. Compared to Istria much of Dalmatia's tourist industry is pleasantly low key as Tito concentrated holiday development further north, leaving large parts of Dalmatia untouched. There is plenty to see in a region where the only constants are outstanding scenery, rich layers of history and the omnipresent waters of the Adriatic.

Northern Dalmatia

During the Homeland War **Zadar** was cut off from the rest of the country as Serb forces pummelled the historic centre. Today the city is getting back on its feet, and the strong sense of civic pride and determination that was so much in evidence during the war is manifesting itself in cultural events, new cafés and an attempt to win the tourists it deserves with its bountiful historic buildings.

Zadar's old town is spectacularly situated on a peninsula, its sturdy walls and lofty gates protecting it from attack. **Široka Ulica**, the arrow-straight Roman road that dissects the old town, passes many of the key sights as it makes its way west to the Adriatic. The post-World War II buildings which replaced those destroyed by Allied bombs are all too evident, but amid them is the baroque church of **St Simeon**, whose treasure is the Romanesque sarcophagus by the Milanese goldsmith Francesco da Sesto, embellished with reliefs depicting the life of the saint and the rescue of his relics from the Venetians by Louis I.

St Donat's Church in Zadar

Further west is **Narodni Trg**, the square that took over from the Roman Forum as the hub of city life during the Middle Ages. Fronting the square is a Venetian-era **Town Loggia** (open Mon–Fri 9am–noon, 5–8pm, Sat 9am–1pm; free), housing an art gallery and temporary exhibitions. Also on the square is the 16th-century Guard House with its lofty clock tower, as well as a couple of pavement cafés. From Narodni Trg it is possible to head north through the old Sea Gate and across a footbridge to the newer part of the city.

A 10-minute walk west along Široka Ulica from Narodni Trg brings you to the site of the Roman Forum. Here, among the stony remains of what was once Zadar's focal point, stands the city's symbol, **St Donat's Church** (opening times vary: high season 9am–10pm, mid-season 9am–1pm, 4–7pm; admission fee). The cylindrical church was built in the 9th century using, in part, stones culled from the Roman Forum, which can be recognised by their Latin inscriptions. The compact two-storey interior, with its tightly packed stone walls, is unlike that of any other religious building in Croatia. Today it no longer functions as a place of worship, but in summer its fine acoustics can be appreciated when it is used as a venue for classical and folk music concerts.

Facing St Donat's Church across the Forum is the worthwhile **Archaeological Museum** (open Mon–Sat 9am–1pm and 5–7pm; admission fee). On display are finds from excavations all over northern Dalmatia, with the Roman era in Zadar well represented.

Zadar Cathedral, on the northwestern side of the Forum, dates from the 12th century, although much on view today was painstakingly reconstructed after Allied bombing during World War II. The slightly incongruous looking bell-tower was

Lacemakers ply their craft in Zadar

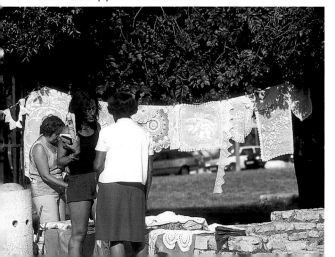

a 19th-century addition to the Romanesque cathedral.

Zadar's newest attraction is the popular **Sea Organ**, built in 2005 on the Riva promenade beside the cruiser port. The 'organ' consists of a series of stone steps leading into the sea, with underwater pipes creating the sound effects. On summer evenings, people gather here to watch the sunset

Estuary crossing at Šibenik

while listening to an ever-changing symphony of nature.

About an hour's drive south of Zadar along the E65 is the city of **Šibenik**. Until the 1990s it was a major industrial centre, but Serb shelling and the resultant disruption to the economy put paid to the traditional enterprises and the city is now one of the poorest in the country. Unusually for the Croatian coastline, there are no traces of Roman civilisation here as the city was established by the Croatian kings a millennium ago. Hence the jumbled streets of the old town and the low-rise muddle of houses that are in contrast to the elegant order of Roman Poreč or Zadar.

The city's main attraction is **Šibenik Cathedral** (open daily 9am–7pm; free), a UNESCO World Heritage Site. Much of the cathedral was the work of Zadar-born Juraj Dalmatinac (*circa* 1400–73), though it took over a century to build and has many different influences incorporated into its grand design, from late-Gothic to Renaissance. The interior is dramatic and engaging, but in many ways it is most impressive for the way in which it dominates the city centre. A good way to appreciate the cathedral's scale is from the café nestling in its shadow on the other side of the square.

An hour's drive south along the E65 past the resort of Primošten is **Trogir**, which also features on UNESCO's World Heritage list, and justifiably so. Trogir's residents like to refer to the old quarter as the 'Town Museum', as it is a beautifully preserved medieval oasis set on its own islet. Much of Trogir still comprises 14th- and 15th-century buildings that in season are very much alive with holidaymakers thronging the old streets, relaxing in the seafood restaurants and embarking on the boat trips that operate from its waterfront.

Trogir's most impressive attraction is its **cathedral** (open high season 8am–7pm, low season 8am–noon, 3–6pm; free). The remarkable 13th-century west portal is the work of Croatian sculptor Master Radovan. The portal depicts scenes from the life of Christ as well as images of local Dalmatian life, including hunting and fishing. In keeping with the political machinations of the time, Jewish and Ottoman figures bear the weight of the portal on their shoulders. Inside is the superb Renaissance Chapel of St John, created by Nikola Firentinac, with its 160 sculpted heads of angels, cherubs and saints.

An easy day trip from Zadar, Šibenik or Trogir is **Krka National Park** (admission fee includes boat ride from Skradin to Skradinski Buk; <www.npkrka.hr>), located inland from Šibenik. This natural wonderland of gorges and waterfalls on the River Krka may be lesser known than the Plitvice Lakes further north, but it is every bit as appealing and not usually as busy. From the village of **Skradin**, 16km (10 miles) from Šibenik, regular boats leave for the impressive **Skradinski Buk** and its 17 separate falls. From Skradinski Buk additional cruises venture deeper into the park (additional fee). **Visovac**, with its Franciscan monastery set in the midst of Visovačko Lake, is alone worth the trip. Housed in the monastery's library is an ornately illustrated copy of *Aesop's Fables*, thought to be one of only three of its kind in the world. Most cruises continue on to **Roški Slap**, another waterfall.

Trogir's immaculate waterfront

Another highlight of Northern Dalmatia is the **Kornati Islands National Park**, <www.kornati.hr>. George Bernard Shaw, the Irish dramatist, eulogised dreamily when he said: 'On the last day of the Creation, God desired to crown his work and thus created the Kornati Islands out of tears, stars and breath.' His words hint at the beauty of the 147 barren, inhospitable and waterless strips of rugged rock that make up the archipelago.

Kornat, which stretches some 25km (15 miles) in length and 2.5km (1½ miles) in width, is the largest; others are little more than rugged rocks, their stark terrain shining like beacons against the blue of the Adriatic. The national park is accessible on day trips from many northern Dalmatian towns and resorts, but undoubtedly the best way to savour the archipelago is to spend a week sailing in their protected waters, stopping off at rustic restaurants and secluded bays, and discovering that Shaw's praise was utterly deserved.

Southern Dalmatia: Split

Dalmatia's largest city, with around 200,000 inhabitants, is **Split**. It was founded by the Roman emperor Diocletian in AD295, and it was here that the Dalmatian-born ruler built his retirement palace between the mountains and the Adriatic. The remarkably intact complex of **Diocletian's Palace** – a UNESCO World Heritage Site – still forms the core of the city. Many of the original palace buildings have long since gone, although remnants of the basement rooms can be seen. Today, cafés, bars, shops and apartments jostle for space within the palace's protective outer walls, which enclose the old town.

Among the places worth visiting in the palace complex is the octagonal **Cathedral of St Domnius** (Sv Duje Katedrala; open daily high season 8am–8pm, low season Mon–Sat 8am–noon and 4–7pm), which was originally built as Diocletian's mausoleum but later converted into a church.

Café in the Peristyle, Diocletian's Palace

A black granite Egyptian sphinx that once sat at the entrance to the mausoleum can be seen to the right of the doorway. The cathedral's wooden doors were carved in 1214 by Andrija Buvina, a local sculptor, and depict scenes from the Life of Christ. You can climb the Romanesque bell-tower (admission fee) for a bird's-eye view of the town.

Guarding the Cathedral of St Domnius

The cathedral overlooks the **Peristyle**, a colonnaded sunken square housing a café that offers an atmospheric setting for refreshment.

North of Diocletian's Palace, through the **Golden Gate** (Zlatna Vrata), which originally led to the Roman town of Salona *(see page 68)*, is the monumental sculpture of the 10th-century bishop, Grgur of Nin (Gregory of Nin) by Ivan Meštrović (1929). Tradition claims that if you touch the statue's toe, a wish will be granted – the said toe is now a golden colour, burnished over the years by the hands of passers by.

For an insight into the life and work of the Split-born sculptor, the **Meštrović Gallery** (Galerija Meštrovića; 46 Šetalište Ivana Meštrovića; open high season Tues–Sun 9am–9pm, low season Tues–Sat 9am–4pm, Sun 10am–3pm; admission fee), situated beneath the Marjan peninsula to the west of the town, features some of his most important work. It is housed in what was the sculptor's summer home.

Split is known for its vibrant nightlife, which centres on Diocletian's Palace until 10pm, after which, in summer, the bars and clubs that line the waterfront to the south become the focal point. Earlier in the evening, locals of all ages like to promenade along **Marmontova**, browsing in its clothes shops, then stopping off at one of the many open-air cafés that line the Riva (seafront promenade).

About 5km (3 miles) inland from Split and accessible by local bus, are the ruins of the once thriving Roman town of **Salona** (open June–Sept Mon–Fri 7am–7pm, Sat 10am–7pm, Sun 4–7pm, Oct–May Mon–Fri 9am–3pm, Sat 9am–2pm; admission fee). Diocletian was born near Salona and it was on account of his affection for the place that he built his palatial home in nearby Split. As the attacks of the Slavs in the 7th century took their toll on Salona the citizens fled to Diocletian's Palace, thus ensuring its survival and the life that today still bustles within its stone walls. A number of remains dot the landscape of Salona and it is possible to trace the original shape of the city and various structures, such as the amphitheatre that in its heyday played host to a baying 18,000-strong crowd.

South of Split

South from Split along the Jadranska Magistrala (Adriatic Highway), the resorts of the **Makarska Riviera** soon appear, tumbling down the hillside from the road towards the pine-fringed Adriatic beaches. Rising above the water to the north are the shadowy peaks of the Biokovo Mountains, which are popular with hikers and climbers, while offshore the Dalmatian islands of Brač and Hvar laze in the Adriatic sun. Such glorious scenery makes up for the somewhat bland towns, ugly developments and the numerous campsites along this stretch of coast.

The most attractive of the resorts is **Brela**, at the northern end of the Riviera.

Trip to Bosnia

In 2001 the railway service from the Croatian port of Ploče to Bosnia recommenced. Adventurous rail travellers can now venture north across the border to Mostar and the capital, Sarajevo.

Split is a good springboard for the Dalmatian Islands

Makarska itself is a big, brash place with good shingle beaches nearby and a vibrant nightlife scene. Resorts to the south include **Tučepi**, **Podgora**, **Drvenik**, and **Zaostrog**; like Makarska, they are geared towards mass-market tourism.

South of Makarska the Magistrala road takes a brief sojourn through Bosnia (note that passports may be checked here), before re-emerging into Croatia and dropping down towards the **Pelješac Peninsula**. This unspoilt spit of land juts out into the Adriatic Sea and provides some of the best wines in Croatia, such as *Dingač* and *Postup*, as well as first-rate seafood. **Ston** is on the mainland side of the peninsula, on the road south towards Dubrovnik. It is well worth breaking the journey here or making a special trip from Dubrovnik to savour the oysters and mussels that are farmed in front of the restaurants on the waterfront. The ultimate tribute to the quality of Ston's culinary fare is that many Italian gastronomes are now making pilgrimages to its restaurants and staying at its few hotels.

Dubrovnik

Widely considered to be one of Europe's most outstanding cities, **Dubrovnik** is an integrated walled city with immense visual appeal. Its historical and architectural significance has been recognised by UNESCO, which has placed it on its list of World Heritage sites. During the Homeland War the city was under siege for six months and the tourist industry was decimated. Now, however, the city has the opposite problem of too many visitors, many of whom are on day trips from the resorts or on cruises. In summer, the old town is very congested, and those turning up without somewhere to stay will almost certainly be disappointed.

The old town of Dubrovnik centring on the cathedral and Rector's Palace

The city's history has been shaped by its perpetual struggle to retain its independence. Settlement in the area first took root in the 7th century when Dubrovnik was an island cut off from the mainland by a small channel. Its original name of Ragusa translates as 'rock' and the former moniker still appears on flags and museums in the city. Even today its citizens are proud that Dubrovnik's sturdy fortifications have never been breached, though in truth the city owed its freedom more to the skill of its diplomats than to its military strength. For centuries the city was a major trading centre, with ships flitting all over the Mediterranean and beyond; by the 15th century its boundaries extended as far as Ston to the north and to Cavtat in the south.

In 1667 a massive earthquake ripped through the region. The damage to Dubrovnik was devastating, with the old core of the city, including its fine Renaissance buildings, practically levelled and over 5,000 people killed. The rebuilding programme was fortunately carefully managed, resulting in the fine baroque centre that we see today. But the city never really regained its former strength as a trading power and at the beginning of the 19th century came under the influence of Napoleonic France. The city declined into a sleepy backwater until the 20th century, when tourists first started taking an interest. Today, the city's tourist industry is as slick and good at making money as its merchants were in the 16th century.

To get a real feel for Dubrovnik, you need to take to the **medieval walls** (open May–Sept 9am–7pm, Oct–Apr 10am–3pm; admission fee) that envelop the old town, opening up vignettes of local life and providing a bird's-eye view of all of the main attractions. The climb is quite steep in parts as the sturdy walls rise up the hillside from the **Pile Gate**, the main entrance to the city, before running along a ridge and descending down past the **Ploče Gate**. The southern walls plunge towards the Adriatic and make for great photos at sunset, when the orange hues of the old town and the stark walls contrast with the blue of the sea.

The streets rise steeply from the north side of Stradun

The **Stradun**, also known as the Placa, is the polished artery that runs through the heart of Dubrovnik with sights to the left and right and a sprinkling of pleasant pavement cafés. Its smooth surface and carefully colour-co-ordinated lampposts seem a far cry from the bitter siege of 1991–2 when Serb forces shelled the residents of the old town. Prijeko, the narrow street running parallel to the Stradun, becomes an almost continuous line of restaurants in season, their tables packed with diners and their colourful owners bellowing for custom.

At the western extremity of the Stradun is the **Big Fountain of Onofrio**, the culmination of a system that has brought fresh water to the city since 1444. The circular domed well, with its 16 water-spouting stone heads, is named after its designer Onofrio della Cava, an Italian who worked in the Dubrovnik region. According to some, it is lucky to drink at the well, but it was originally intended merely for washing on entering the city. A more minor fountain,

Catch a ferry from the Old Port to Lokrum island

known as the **Small Fountain of Onofrio**, lies near the church of St Blaise *(see page 74)*.

To the east, the Stradun leads to **Luža Square**, site of a cluster of historic buildings. The 16th-century **Sponza Palace** (open high season Mon–Fri 8am–3pm, Sat 8am–1pm, low season Mon–Fri 8am–1pm; admission fee) served as a bank, customs house, mint and treasury, before its current role as home to the state archives. This remarkable collection records the history and administration of Ragusa from the 13th century until its fall at the beginning of the 19th century. A shop selling facsimiles of historical documents is found in the palace's courtyard, as is the Memorial Room to the Defenders of Dubrovnik, with portraits of those who died during the 1991–2 siege. The courtyard is an atmospheric venue for musical performances during the Dubrovnik Festival in August.

At the southern end of Luža Square stands **Orlando's Column** (also known as Roland's Column) dating from

The Rector's Palace

1418. It commemorates a mysterious figure who is said to have helped fight off Saracen pirates in the 8th century and in doing so earned the city's eternal gratitude. Orlando continues to play his part in Dubrovnik life as his column is where the start of the Dubrovnik Festival is declared every year.

Opposite is the 18th-century church of **St Blaise** (Crkva Sv Vlaho), named after the patron saint of Dubrovnik. Above the high altar stands a silver figure of St Blaise holding a scale model of the city: look out for similar representations of the saint elsewhere in the city.

A short walk from the church is the **Rector's Palace** (Knežev Dvor; open summer daily 9am–6pm, winter Mon–Sat 9am–2pm; admission fee). This palatial building is a fitting residence for a figure who, in theory at least, was the most powerful person in the city. However, the honour of being rector was modified slightly by the fact that his family was not allowed to live with him and he was forbidden from leaving the palace unless on official business.

Constructed in the mid-15th century, the palace was the seat of the Ragusan government as well as housing a lethal gunpowder store that ignited with devastating effect on a couple of occasions. The present building dates mainly from 1739 and is in baroque style with a few Gothic details. On the ground floor of the palace are prison cells and on the upper floor are the state apartments and the former courtroom and judicial chambers. The palace's atrium makes a lovely concert venue.

Nearby is the **cathedral** (open daily 8am–7pm) which was almost totally destroyed by the earthquake of 1667. The interior comes alive with dramatic celebrations of Mass and classical concerts during the Dubrovnik Festival. Note the compelling *Assumption* by Titian on the main altar. The adjoining treasury (admission fee) displays a horde of gold reliquaries, including the Byzantine skull case of St Blaise. A local legend tells of how Richard the Lionheart was saved from a shipwreck while returning from the Crusades and by way of thanks funded the building of the first cathedral.

In a narrow side street between the Stradun and Prijeko, near Pile Gate, **War Photo Limited** (open June–Sept daily 9am–9pm, May and Oct Tues–Sat 10am–4pm and Sun 10am–2pm; admission fee; <www.warphotoltd.com>) is a slick gallery devoted to photo-journalism from war zones around the world.

Most of Dubrovnik's other sites lie in the very compact area inside the city walls, mostly off the Stradun or Luža Square. They include the Franciscan and Dominican monasteries, the Maritime Museum, the Rupe Granary (housing the Ethnographic Museum), the Jesuit Church and the city's synagogue.

The best time of year to visit the city is during the **Dubrovnik Festival**, held mid-July to mid-August. This arts extravaganza features theatre, opera and musical performances, and many historical buildings are opened as venues. Booking tickets in advance is essential: <www.dubrovnik-festival.hr>.

Those with a few days in Dubrovnik may want to make a refreshing trip over to the island of **Lokrum**, just offshore. In high season regular boats make the short crossing. The main pleasures are lazing around on the beaches, strolling through the shady woodland and visiting its monastery, botanical garden and the modest remains of Napoleonic fortifications.

Dalmatian Islands

The city of Split is a good base for exploring the Dalmatian Islands, offering regular ferry connections. Just half an hour across the water is **Brač**, Croatia's third largest island and the location of **Žlatni Rat** (Golden Cape) near Bol. This shingle peninsula cuts scenically into the Adriatic, attracting countless sun-worshippers and boat cruises during summer. Bol itself has a pleasant old town and is a centre for walks in the surrounding hills; it is also one of the best places in Croatia for windsurfing.

The neighbouring island of **Hvar** is a favourite with wealthy Croatians and also Italians, who take advantage of the direct

Brač's Zlatni Rat (Golden Cape) has some of the best beaches in Croatia

ferry services from Italy during the high season. The unassuming town of Stari Grad, with its new ferry terminal, is where most visitors arrive, but **Hvar Town** is the real star. Here, amid wild lavender (for which the island is famous) and rosemary, palaces and churches financed by rich Venetian merchants scatter the hillside. Lined with pavement cafés and restaurants, the Riva is the central thoroughfare, leading from the busy little harbour to the 16th-century St Stephen's Cathedral which dominates the main square.

Vis is the furthest island from the Croatian mainland and is quite unlike any of the others. It was first populated by the Greeks in the 4th century BC. Many of Europe's major powers have fought over it down the centuries including Austria, Italy, Germany and Britain, the latter two during World War II. Tourism was restricted here until 1989, as the island was used as a Yugoslav naval base.

Vis Town curves around a bay with its most appealing quarter, Kut, where wealthy Venetians built their homes during the 16th century. The Franciscan monastery

Tito's HQ

Tito set up base in a cave on Vis during World War II. From here he conducted many military operations and also hosted Churchill's envoy.

features gravestones by the celebrated Croatian sculptor, Ivan Rendić (1849–1932), as well as a mass grave for Austrian sailors killed in a sea battle off Vis in 1866.

Across the mountains from Vis Town is the fishing village of **Komiža**. As you approach, the church of St Nicholas, on a vine-covered bluff, offers a shady respite from the summer heat; its nearby cemetery contains the ornate tombs of notable local families. In Komiža itself there is a modest **Maritime Museum** (open summer only 9am–noon, 7–10pm; admission fee) that testifies to the town's fruitful association with the Adriatic. But the main reason for coming to Komiža is to take a boat trip or go scuba diving at the offshore island of **Biševo**, where, during summer, the Blue Cave (Modra Špilja) is illuminated by a brilliant blue light, similar to the celebrated Blue Cave off Capri. Numerous boat trips run out to the cave from Komiža.

Further along the coastline, the island of **Korčula** perches on the western end of the Pelješac Peninsula *(see page 69)*. **Korčula Town** is one of the most attractive settlements on the coastline, jutting out from the mountains on its own peninsula. It can be visited on a lengthy day trip from Dubrovnik, but is also an excellent place to spend a few days. Surrounded by solid medieval walls, the old town is laid out

Moreška Dance

Korčula is the birthplace of Croatia's traditional dance, the Moreška, dating from the 15th century. A predictable story of good and evil, it dramatises the battle of two kings, the white and the black, who fight to woo the favours of a fair maiden. Performances (Monday and Thursday in high season) are held in the small outdoor theatre in Korčula Town. The most important Moreška of the year is performed on July 27 on the feast of St Theodore.

Floating in the crystal-clear waters of Mljet National Park

on a tight grid system. The locals claim that the legendary explorer Marco Polo hails from the town, and you can visit the **Marco Polo House** (open high season only 9am–7pm; admission fee) where the explorer is said to have been born. **St Mark's Cathedral** combines Gothic and Renaissance styles and contains an *Annunciation* by Tintoretto, who spent time in Korčula as a student.

South towards Dubrovnik the island of **Mljet** is often overlooked, but not by Croatians who are very aware of the beauty of this green and lush island. The **Mljet National Park**, <www.np-mljet.hr>, centres upon two beautiful lakes, Malo Jerezo (small lake) and Veliko Jerezo (big lake), which are excellent for swimming, with crystal clear water and the shade of evergreen forests on the water's edge. There is a cycling path around one of the lakes and it is possible to go on a boat trip out to **St Mary's Island** to visit its **monastery**, an atmospheric spot with a restaurant and café.

WHAT TO DO

There is no shortage of activities on offer in Croatia. If you're looking for something adventurous, the Adriatic coast is a paradise for scuba diving, sailing and other watersports. Inland you can go rafting and canoeing on the rivers or hiking and climbing in the mountains. There are beaches to relax on, islands to discover and historic walled cities to explore. Festivals give insights into local arts and culture; shopping, entertainment and nightlife are all to be enjoyed.

SPORTS

Diving

Croatia is rapidly emerging as one of Europe's top scuba diving destinations. There are dive centres all the way along the Croatian coastline from Umag and Rovinj in Istria to Dubrovnik in southern Dalmatia.

The highlight for many divers is the island of Vis, which has several diveable shipwrecks just off its coast. A short boat ride away is the Blue Grotto at Biševo, where in summer a unique phenomenon casts ultra blue light into the small grotto, making for a memorable spectacle, best seen from under the water.

Other favourite destinations for divers are the Kornati Islands, Mezanj Island near Dugi Otok, Rovinj and, to the south, the shipwreck of the *Tottono*, which was lost off the Dalmatian coast near Dubrovnik during World War II.

Scuba diving is strictly regulated in Croatia and no one is allowed to dive without first obtaining a diving certificate, which costs 100kn. The certificate is valid for one year from the date of issue and allows qualified divers to dive in any permitted area up to a depth of 40m (130ft). Proof that divers have already passed an internationally recognised dive course such as SSI, CMAS and PADI must be provided. Courses lasting a week are available for beginners.

Pro Diving Croatia can provide more information. Its website <www.diving.hr> features information on getting a dive certificate and also the locations of the various dive centres.

Sailing

Croatia is emerging as something of an oasis for yachting enthusiasts, with Bill Gates, Bernie Ecclestone and Luciano Benetton said to be among those now cruising around its Adriatic coastline in summer. Areas such as the sheltered Kornati Islands are great for those who are learning the ropes, while more adventurous sailing awaits those who venture further out to sea where the local *bura* and *yugo* winds are a test even for the most experienced sailors.

There are 50 marinas along the coast from Umag in the north of Istria to Cavtat in the very south of the country. Adriatic Croatian International (ACI; <www.aci-club.hr>) are the biggest operator with 21 marinas. Some of the larger marinas are almost resorts in themselves, while others, such as those at Trogir and Rab, bring you right into the heart of the town.

Would-be sailors have the choice of going 'bareboat' by just chartering a boat themselves, or taking a skipper. For bareboat you will need at least one member of your party to be a qualified skipper who can use a VHF radio. If you choose the skippered option the cost goes up and you have to take one less person along in your party as the hired skipper will also sleep aboard. The toughest parts of sailing, such as navigation, will be taken out of your hands, though you and other members of your party will be required to help out with the ropes.

Wind-surfing is good at Bol on the Dalmatian island of Hvar

The website of the Croatian National Tourist Office <www.croatia.hr> has a comprehensive section on sailing with links for further information.

Other watersports

All the coastal resorts offer watersports, especially in Istria where larger hotels lay on everything from water-skiing to parasailing. Or you can simply go snorkelling in the crystal clear Adriatic. Inland, the rivers Kupa and Cetina are suitable for both rafting and canoeing. Organised rafting trips set off regularly in season, subject to conditions.

Football

The most popular spectator sport in Croatia is undoubtedly football, in which the country has an impressive record, achieving third place at the World Cup in 1998 only seven years after declaring independence. The Croatian national team play most of their games at the Maksimir Stadium in Zagreb, but also sometimes travel to Split and Varaždin. Dinamo Zagreb also play at Maksimir, regularly doing well in their domestic league and also playing in the UEFA Champions League where they have faced the likes of Manchester United. Their great rivals have always been Hadjuk Split from the southern city and big games between the two can be turbulent affairs. Varteks, from Varaždin, have in recent years also been emerging as a major force.

Tennis

The other major spectator sport in Croatia is tennis, with major players such as Ivan Ljubičić and his compatriot Mario Ančić drawing big crowds for their matches. The highlight of the tennis calendar is in July in Umag when the Croatian Tennis Open regularly attracts big names to an event that is

Rock-climbing in Paklenica National Park

becoming more popular every year.

There are also plenty of opportunities to play tennis. Every major coastal resort has tennis courts, and while many are affiliated to hotels, non-residents can also usually arrange a game for a fee. The excellent facilities at Umag host the Croatian Tennis Open, but when they are not in use for tournaments or training, they can be rented out, offering a rare chance for amateurs to play at a major venue.

Rafting

Whitewater rafting is possible on several of Croatia's rivers. The Kupa River, near Karlovac, offers some of the best rafting in Central Croatia. Towards the Adriatic, in the Gorski Kotar, rafting can be arranged on the Dobra River. From the Dalmatian coast it is easy to get to the Cetina River, where rafting can be enjoyed in spring and summer.

Walking, Hiking and Climbing

Croatia has a range of opportunities for walking and hiking. The most popular areas with mountaineers and those looking for a real challenge are the Velebit range and the sheer limestone walls of Paklenica National Park. The park has basic facilities and caters for all levels of climber, from beginner right through to serious mountaineers and daredevil freeclimbers. At the entrance to the main gorge a steep rock wall is used for practising, training and for showing first-timers the ropes.

Elsewhere, the Risnjak National Park at the northern end of the Velebit is more suited to those intending to trek and hike. On the eastern edge of the Istrian peninsula, where it meets the Kvarner Gulf, Mt Učka is good for day trips from the resorts of Opatija and Labin. Southwest of Zagreb are the Samobor Hills where Tito first laced up his hiking boots.

SHOPPING

Croatia is not normally considered a great shopping destination, but visitors will be pleasantly surprised. The cities, especially Zagreb, have a good range of designer stores and interesting shops. Nearly everything is available here that you would find in any other major European city. The towns and villages have smaller outlets selling local produce and handicrafts, and in the coastal resorts the work of local artists is on sale.

Best Buys
Food and Drink

In Croatia some locals refer to any food that is not organic as 'chicken feed', such is the prevalence of organic produce throughout the country. Under communism much of the country's food was produced on a local small-scale or family basis and as a result the people take great pride in the quality and high standard of their produce.

Often the best places to buy the freshest fruit and vegetables are the bountiful local markets, still very much alive

Truffles

Istria is the place to be for truffle lovers. The region's interior is one of Europe's most productive regions for truffle hunting. One of the best places to purchase truffle products is Zigante Tartufi, <www.zigantetartufi.com>. This retail group, which stakes claim to having found the world's biggest truffle, sells its white truffles, black truffles, truffle oil and truffled sheep cheese throughout Istria. They have branches at Smareglina 7 in Pula (tel: 052-214855), J.B. Tita 12 in Buje (tel: 052-772125), Trg Fontana in Buzet (tel: 052-663340) and Livade 7 in Livade, where an excellent restaurant serves truffle dishes (tel: 052-664030).

Flavoured oils and honey for sale by a road in Istria

today despite the increasing number of shopping malls and supermarkets. Most markets in Croatia are open Monday–Saturday 8am–2pm, and many also work Sunday 8–11am. Markets in the holiday resorts also sell souvenirs; as a result, they tend to have extended opening hours.

Food items to look out for are *paški sir*, the excellent salty sheep cheese from the North Dalmatian island of Pag, as well as the delicious Pršut smoked ham, which is served in thin slices all along the coastline, but particularly in Dalmatia. Croatian olive oil is also highly rated, as are its truffles, which are found in the Istrian interior. Kulen sausage from Slavonia is a spicy and tasty treat that travels well.

Croatia is also gaining a reputation for its wines, with a multitude of varieties available. Istria and Dalmatia produce the best known and most highly regarded wines, but family-run and larger vineyards can be found all over the country. Wine is disproportionately expensive in the country due to high production costs and the relatively small domestic market, but the quality is high. There is an increasing number of specialist wine shops, especially in the resorts.

Jewellery and Clothes

Items of jewellery, especially silver pieces and necklaces made from Adriatic coral, can be found in all of the coastal resorts in summer, sold from small shops or temporary stalls. The jewellery is often made in the outlying villages. Hand-made silk neckties *(kravata)* are also popular, as is lace from the island of Pag, where the local women have made it by hand for centuries. From Rijeka comes the distinctive traditional *morčić* jewellery.

Souvenir-hunting in Dubrovnik

Designer fashion can be found in Zagreb. In Croatia's second city, Split, clothes shopping is a joy, as there are a number of small shops in and around Diocletian's Palace, which provides a dramatic setting for retail therapy. The citizens of Split are among the best dressed people in the country and though prices are not cheap, quality is high with bespoke items still good value.

Arts and Crafts

Over recent years the arts and crafts scene in Croatia has really developed. Most tourists encounter it in the coastal resorts in the form of skyline depictions of the historic sights. More interesting are the individual paintings and artworks found in small shops in towns such as Grožnjan and Rovinj.

Lavender, a product of Hvar

Where to Shop

Zagreb has a multitude of shops selling the latest fashions and designer clothes. The heart of the action is on the grand thoroughfare of Ilica and its surrounding streets. Gharani Štrok Boutique (Dežmanova Prolaz 5; tel: 01-4846152) stocks clothes, shoes and jewellery designed by the London-based company of the same name – the co-founder, Vanya Štrok, was born in Croatia and moved to London at the age of 11. Alternatively, Croata (Ilica 5; tel: 01-4812726) specialises in Croatian ties.

The best place to purchase Croatian wines, *rakija* olive oil and truffle products is Vinoteka Bornstein (Kaptol 19; tel: 01-4812363), located in a large brick cellar close to the cathedral.

For an extensive choice of English-language books, call at Algoritam (Gajeva 1) just off the main square.

Shopping centres in the capital include Centar Kaptol (Nova Ves 17), Importanne (Starčević Trg) and Mercatone (Gospodarska Ulica).

In Split, Diocletian's Palace is *the* place to shop, where a number of small domestic designers and international names have their outlets. At the western end of the palace is the shining Marmontova that sweeps seawards in a flashy array of European high-street stores and trendy boutiques. Shopping is at its busiest during early evening when the local smart set are out to see and be seen.

In Dubrovnik, several small, select wine stores have opened in the old town, the best being Dubrovačka Kuča (Svetog Dominika; tel: 020-322092), close to Ploče Gate, which stocks a wide choice of Croatian wines and *rakija*, and has an art gallery selling tasteful paintings by local artists.

In Istria, Poreč's charming Ulica Decumanus, where one-time Roman town houses and Venetian villas brim with tourist shops, is a good place to look for souvenirs.

Further north, Rovinj's Ulica Grisia is a pretty street given over to small arts and crafts shops. Arguably the best place to purchase original art in Croatia is in the Istrian hill town of Grožnjan, a government-sponsored community of artists.

ENTERTAINMENT

In the summer months the Croatian coastline can be as lively and energetic at night as most other places in the Mediterranean with the old cabaret-and-tacky-disco scene being rapidly replaced by stylish cocktail bars and buzzing clubs. There is a good sprinkling of bars and clubs in all the big coastal resorts, though out of season many close down. The same happens to some of Zagreb's venues during the summer, when many of the locals depart to the coast.

The terms bar and café can be interchangeable in Croatia and relaxed licensing laws mean that most are open between 7am and midnight, while some do not close until 2am or when the crowds disperse.

In Zagreb the place to see and be seen is Tkalčićeva, a winding lane on the border between the Gornji Grad and

Night on the tiles

Outdoor nightlife begins in April and culminates in July and August, when festivals offer outdoor cultural entertainment. The islands offer most fun for the young, especially in Novalja on Pag and Jelsa on Hvar.

Folk performance in the Rector's Palace, Dubrovnik

Donji Grad. When weather allows, this party oasis attracts the local smart set, who idle the night away in pavement cafés.

Outside the capital, other notable bars and clubs include Valentino Café in Rovinj (Sv. Križa 28), with its mellow music and cushions on the rocks, from which you can watch the sun setting over the Adriatic, and Zanzibar (Budicina bb), a fashionable bar with comfortable seating and a large terrace.

In Rijeka look out for Hemingway, formerly known as Filodrammatica (Korzo 28), a luxurious place with legendary hot chocolate.

In Dubrovnik, Jazz Caffè Troubador (Bunićeva Poljana) is a famous jazz bar in the old town. The Café Festival (Stradun) is great for people-watching while enjoying a single malt whisky.

Gheto Klub (Dosud 10) in Split is one of several hip bars on the second level of Diocletian's Palace, while in Zadar The Garden (<www.thegardenzadar.com>) is the place to be, with its leafy setting above the city walls.

Cultural Performances

There is an extensive cultural programme of theatre, opera and classical music in Zagreb and to a lesser extent in the cities of Split, Dubrovnik, Rijeka, Pula, Osijek and Varaždin. Many of the performances form part of the season of summer festivals, but there is usually something on throughout the year in each city. The biggest annual event is the Dubrovnik Summer Festival, held in Dubrovnik from mid-July to mid-August, and featuring theatre, opera, dance and classical music.

Local tourist offices have listings of current and forthcoming events and may also book tickets.

CROATIA FOR CHILDREN

Children are welcomed almost everywhere, but there are not a lot of attractions particularly aimed at children. In Zagreb, the parks make a good escape for younger travellers not bewitched by the city's many museums. Things are better on the coast, where the big resorts have plenty to keep children occupied. The larger hotels have children's clubs, especially in Poreč where families are particularly well catered for.

Kids love the coast

The calm waters of the coast are suitable for supervised children, though look out for jagged rocks and sea urchins. The shallow waters around the Kornati Islands are good for supervised canoeing. Festivals, including the International Children's Festival held in Šibenik in June/July, are also a good source of entertainment for youngsters.

Calendar of Events

Croatia's cultural scene has received a huge boost since independence, with many old festivals resurrected and others given a new lease of life.

3 February Feast of St Blaise, Dubrovnik: gunpowder, religious processions and marching bands for the feast day of Dubrovnik's patron saint.

February Rijeka Carnival: Croatia's third largest city wakes up from its winter slumber in the days preceding Lent.

Late June–early July The International Children's Festival, Šibenik: a mixture of ballet, art and performances by children's theatre groups.

July Zagreb Summer Festival (*Zagrebački Ljetni Festival*): outdoor cultural festival with performances throughout the capital. Zagreb International Folklore Festival: domestic artists are joined by performers from across the Balkans and further afield.

Late July Pula Film Festival: there can be few better settings in the world for a film festival than the ancient Roman amphitheatre.

Early July–mid-August Musical Evenings In St Donat's (*Muzičke večeri u Sv. Donatu*), Zadar: the acoustics of this medieval church are perfect for grand classical performances.

10 July–25 August Dubrovnik Summer Festival (*Dubrovački Ljetni Festival*): the Libertas Festival is rapidly establishing a name for itself as one of Europe's top festivals. Tickets are limited, but catching a performance in one of the city's historical buildings is unforgettable.

July and August The Summer of Split (*Splitsko Ljeto*): a solid programme of cultural events; many of the performances arc in and around the atmospheric Diocletian's Palace. The Summer Events on the Island of Krk: cultural action focuses on Krk Town's atmospheric old town. Istrian Musical and Cultural Summer: Poreč, Umag, Rovinj, Pula and Grožnjan all play host to cultural events and concerts.

Late September Vinkovci Autumn Festival (*Vinkovačke Jeseni*): a two-day national review of authentic Croatian folklore.

Late September–early October Varaždin Baroque Evenings (*Varazdinske Barokne Veceri*): opera and baroque ensembles.

24–25 December Christmas festivities throughout the country.

EATING OUT

Croatia is increasingly being recognised as worth visiting for its food and drink alone. Perhaps the ultimate compliment is that many discerning Italians are now making the journey over the Adriatic every summer in search of some of the best-value seafood in Europe and also to sample the excellent wines that the country produces.

The best seafood restaurants are located along the Adriatic coast, but the cuisine of Slavonia also has its merits, with good river fish and meat dishes that take their influences from Hungary rather than Italy. Zagreb has the greatest choice of restaurants in the country with the cuisine of many nations represented.

When to Eat

In the summer season many restaurants in the resorts stay open all day, serving an identical menu for lunch and dinner, though what is on offer varies depending on the availability of seafood. Traditionally Croatians are early risers, taking a stiff shot of coffee to kick-start the day, perhaps along with a pastry snack. Lunch is normally taken around noon to 2pm, though this can vary along the coast, where in summer many locals live a more Mediterranean lifestyle, with later lunches and siestas. Dinner is usually eaten later than in most Western European countries, with restaurants serving food until around 11pm or even later. Out of season it is common for many restau-

Cheap eats

Eating out is much less common among locals than in many other European countries – mainly on account of cost – but you will find locals eating in pizzerias, which are inexpensive and serve excellent pizza.

rants in the coastal resorts to close down completely.

What to Eat

There is a great deal of regional variation in Croatia, with Italian influences prevailing along the coast, where seafood is the obvious highlight. Inland, meat specialities come to the fore and richer Austrian and Hungarian cooking styles prevail. One common thread is quality, with an emphasis on organic produce and freshness. Fish is usually cooked and eaten on the day it is caught, and all towns and villages have a farmers' market. The fast-food culture and product homogeneity that is found in European Union countries has yet to descend on the country.

Presenting the dish of the day in a small *konoba* in Istria

Starters

A common starter in restaurants all over the country is a plate of ham and cheese accompanied by bread. Usually it is the smoked ham known as *pršut*, which is produced in Istria and Dalmatia and at its best is every bit as good as Spain's *jamon serrano* and Italy's *prosciutto*. The most renowned cheese is *paški sir*, a salty variety produced on the island of Pag. You can ask for a plate of freshly sliced tomatoes as an accompaniment.

Seafood starters are also good. Highlights include *salata od hobotnice* (octopus salad with olive oil), *ligne* (squid) or the more expensive *salata od jastoga* (pieces of lobster marinated in herbs and olive oil). In Slavonia and inland hearty soups are also common – look out for *fiš paprikaš* from Slavonia, a spicy stew of river fish such as pike, catfish and carp, and *fažol*, a hearty peasant bean stew from Istria. Mushrooms are also used a lot, notably in Istria, which is also the centre of the truffle industry *(see page 86).*

Fish and Seafood

Croatia's range of seafood is extensive. There are numerous highlights, but one inexpensive and unfussy dish that sustains many travellers is *rižot frutti di mare* (seafood risotto), which is both tasty and filling. Croatians like to let their seafood speak for itself and there are few complicated French-style sauces here. Most dishes come *na žaru* (grilled), *lešu* (boiled) or *u pećinici* (baked). The best fish is sold by

Octopus salad, a popular starter on the coast

weight and at the top restaurants it will be brought out for you to inspect first. Among the bountiful stock in the Adriatic are *list* (sole), *kovač* (John Dory) and *trilja* (red mullet).

Shellfish are also very popular and of high quality, especially around the Pelješac Peninsula and the town of Ston. Look out for huge *oštrige* (oysters) and *dagnje* (mussels), the latter sometimes coming with a *buzara* sauce, reminiscent of *moules marinières* with garlic and white wine. *Jastog* (lobster) is expensive compared to other options, but still very good value. The *škampi* (prawns) are often served whole, simply grilled or in a *buzara* sauce.

Meat

On the coast meat dishes are usually limited to grilled beef and pork, but head inland and it is a different story. Between the coast and Zagreb the hills are dotted with small restaurants that specialise in spit-roasted lamb and pork. You can tell which places are open by the pigs and lambs slowly turning over the hot coals outside. This fatty delicacy is usually served unadorned and accompanied by a few chunks of bread and a simple salad.

In terms of fast food, the ubiquitous *ćevapčići* is much beloved of many Croats, especially the younger generations. These spicy meatballs are succulent and tasty, and usually come with a salad and bread, making a quick, filling lunch option.

The Austrian influence comes through in the Zagorje region north of the capital, where *schnitzels* are omnipresent on menus, while Zagreb even has its own version, the *Zagrebački odrezak*, which comes stuffed with cheese and ham. In Slavonia, to the east of the capital, the Hungarian influences bring in spicy paprika and hearty stews such as *gulaš*. A highlight here is the fine *kulen* sausage, a large and spicy affair not dissimilar to Spanish *chorizo*, which is eaten on its own with bread and used in stews.

Desserts

Ice cream *(sladoled)* is superb in Croatia, rivalling Italian *gelati* in its taste and quality. No hot Adriatic summer's day would be complete without at least one, preferably taken before or after dinner when entire resorts take ice-cream fuelled strolls along the waterfront. The range of flavours is impressive, with all the usual fruit and chocolate temptations, as well as the slightly more unusual, recently introduced 'Viagra' flavour.

Croatian desserts do not stop at ice cream. From the town of Samobor comes *kremšnita*, a creamy and delicate custard cake. *Voćna salata* (fruit salad) is a healthy option, and less so are the common *štrudl* (strudel) and *torta* (gateau). Desserts tend to get more calorific as you head inland, again thanks to the influences of Austria and Hungary. *Palačinke* (pancakes) come laden with cream, nuts and seasonal fruits.

For the majority of Croatians, though, dessert is usually just a strong cup of coffee, perhaps followed by an ice cream on a postprandial stroll around town.

A taste of Turkey

Though not as pronounced as in some of the other Balkan countries, Turkish influences are evident, particularly in indigenous fast food such as meat kebabs and *burek* (cheese baked in filo pastry). Among the desserts, you will also find *baklava*, filo pastry smothered in honey and nuts. Turkish coffee, drunk very strong in tiny cups, is popular.

Croatian Wine

Croatia produces a massive array of wines, of varying quality, from simple table white wines that are produced to go with fish dishes, to excellent and robust reds that stand their ground against many wines from France and Italy. To cut costs, Croatians like to drive out to the vineyards

A balancing act in Trogir

and stock up on supplies. Istria and the Samobor Hills near Zagreb are packed with small-scale producers selling direct to customers.

Red Wines. Dingač from the Pelješac Peninsula in southern Dalmatia is regarded as the 'King of Croatian Wines'. This robust 14-percent-proof wine goes well with all meat dishes and is also excellent on its own, although it can be expensive at over 90kn a bottle. Pelješac is also home to the considerably cheaper red Plavac, more often than not served as table wine, though when produced properly it can also stand on its own. Postup is another Pelješac wine that has been compared to American Zinfandel.

Further north in Dalmatia Šibenik produces its own Plavina and Babić wines, as well as an acceptable rosé. Neighbouring Primošten produces its own excellent Babić. Although most production in Istria is of white wine, Teran is a passable red, though it can be overloaded with tannin.

White Wines. In the north more than 70 percent of Istria's production is white wine. Look out for Muscatel and Malvazija. In Southern Dalmatia, tucked on the end of the Pelješac peninsula, is the island of Korčula, which is renowned for its Pošip and the especially good Grk, both varieties of white.

It is thought that wine was first produced in Croatia by the Greeks on the island of Vis. Today Vis has myriad vineyards that specialise in Viški Plavac (red) and Vugava (white), with many small scale operations. Arguably the best of all the island wines is Vrbnička Žlahtina. From the vine-covered slopes around the town of Vrbnik, in the north

A glass of Croatian red

of the Kvarner Gulf island of Krk, this straw-yellow wine is superb and goes particularly well with the local fish dishes; it is also good for drinking on its own on steamy summer nights. A good dessert wine is Prošek, which is the perfect accompaniment to the very sweet desserts.

It is common for locals to dilute their wine with a little water (called a *bevanda*) or add a touch of sparkling mineral water (*gemišt*), with Vrbnička Žlahtina working well in both cases. Connoisseurs may be distressed to see Croatians pouring orange juice into their red wine, but it actually makes for a very refreshing drink when the temperature rises.

Away from the coast Slavonia produces some excellent white wines and, like the local food, these are very distinctive. Two to look out for, as the region recovers from the war damage inflicted on its vineyards, are Graševina and also Kutjevo Chardonnay, which complement the spicy fish dishes of the region.

Other Drinks

Beer *(pivo)* is a popular drink, especially in summer. Foreign import brands are becoming increasingly widespread as producers attempt to saturate the market, but thankfully, for the time being, there is a good range of domestically owned and produced beers. The best of them all, and commonly available, is Karlovaćko, from Karlovac, which has a clean, crisp flavour and a pleasant aftertaste. Its biggest rival is Ožujsko from Zagreb, a heavier tasting lager beer that rewards repeated tastings.

In Slavonia you'll find the less well-known Oziječko, which is an excellent lager. Most visitors tend to avoid Istria's Favorit after their first sample, and with good reason, as it has a slightly metallic flavour and a poor aftertaste.

Domestic spirits are hugely popular and found in most bars and restaurants. They include the fiery grappa digestif, which can be dynamite, especially if it is home-made. *Šljivovica* (plum brandy) is a good digestif, but it can also have quite a kick (beware of getting drawn into a drinking competition on this spirit as Croatians seem to be able to handle it like Russians do vodka, while tourists generally end up collapsing).

Other domestic spirits include *Maraskino*, a cherry liqueur from Zadar, and *Biska*, a mistletoe-based aperitif produced in inland Istria.

To Help You Order...

Could we have a table for…?	**Imate li stol za…?**
Please could you bring…?	**Molim vas donesite…?**
The bill, please	**Račun molim**
menu	**jelovnik**

bread	**kruh**	salad	**salata**
butter	**maslac**	salt	**sol**
coffee	**kava**	sugar	**šećer**
dessert	**deserti**	tea	**čaj**
fish	**riba**	with milk	**s mlijekom**
fruit	**voće**	with lemon	**s limunom**
ice cream	**sladoled**	with rum	**s rumom**
meat	**meso**	wine	**vino**
milk	**mlijeko**	white	**bijelo**
pepper	**papar**	red	**crno**
rice	**riža**	rosé	**roze**

...and Read the Menu

beer	**pivo**	cheese	**sir**
black coffee	**crna kava**	cold meat	**hladno pečenje**
brandy	**rakija**	ham	**šunka**
fruit juice	**voćni sok**	raw,	**sirova**
mineral	**mineralna**	cooked	**kuhana**
water	**voda**	smoked	**dimljena**
plum brandy	**šljivovica**	Parma ham	**pršut**
table wine	**stolno vino**	olives	**masline**
egg	**jaje**	sausage	**kobasica**
ham	**omlet sa**	soup	**juha**
omelette	**sunkom**	cod	**bakalar**
honey	**med**	lobster	**jastog**
jam	**marmelada**	mussels	**dagnje**

shellfish	**školjke**	veal	**teleći**
octopus	**hobotnica**	cutlet	**odrezak**
oyster	**kamenica**	risotto	**rižot**
prawns	**škampi**	truffle	**tartufe**
squid	**lignje**	apple	**jabuka**
beefsteak	**biftek**	banana	**banana**
spicy	**čevapčići**	orange	**naranča**
meatballs		strawberry	**jagoda**
Slavonian	**kulen**	beans	**grah**
sausage		cucumber	**krastavac**
beef	**goveđi**	green	**paprika**
goulash	**gulaš**	pepper	
chicken	**pile**	mushrooms	**gljive**
roast	**pečeni**	onion	**crveni luk**
suckling	**odojak**	potato	**krumpir**
pig on	**na ražnju**	salad	**salata**
the spit		cake	**kolač**
pork chops	**svinjski kotleti**	fruit salad	**voćna salata**
lamb on	**janje na**	pancakes	**palačinka**
the spit	**ražnju**	whipped	**šlag**
turkey	**tuka**	cream	

Restaurant Culture

There are several kinds of restaurant in Croatia. The first is the formal *restoran*, which are plentiful in the big resorts and cities and usually offer international food. More authentic and more likely to provide regional specialities are *konoba* (inns), small family-run restaurants. These often offer dishes of the day and may not even run to a standard menu; the choice varies depending on what is freshest and cheapest at the morning market. The last category are road-side establishments serving succulent spit-roasted pork and lamb with bread and simple salads.

HANDY TRAVEL TIPS

An A–Z Summary of Practical Information

A

ACCOMMODATION

Hotels, apartments, campsites and private accommodation in Croatia are all graded by the government and receive one to five stars. Standards in four- and five-star establishments are consistently high, but there are greater variations in the lower grades.

Hotels. Croatia offers a wide variety of hotels, from clean and functional resort hotels to luxurious business-oriented establishments and intimate boutique hotels *(see pages 128–136)*.

Private accommodation. There is also a wealth of privately owned lodgings available, from basic rooms to exclusive use of apartments. In general, private accommodation can only be booked through local travel agents.

Farmhouses. In Istria the *Agroturizam* programme <www.istra.com/agroturizam> offers visitors the opportunity to stay in a family home or a traditional stone farmhouse in the tranquil Istrian hills, where you can experience a taste of the real Croatia away from the resorts.

Further information on the *Agroturizam* programme can be found at <www.istra.com>, or from the Istria County Tourist Association, tel: 052-452797.

Lighthouses. One of the more unusual accommodation options in Croatia comes in the form of renovated, but still operational lighthouses. Croation Lighthouses <www.lighthouses-croatia.com> can supply information about stays (and online booking) in one of 11 lighthouses located on headlands and islands in Istria and Dalmatia.

I'd like a single/double room	Trebao bih jednokrevetnu sobu/dvokrevetnu sobu
with bath/shower	sa banjom/tušem
What's the rate per night?	Koliko košta za jednu noć?

Campsites. Croatia also has a large number of campsites called *autocamps*, most of which are graded as three-star and have excellent amenities and numerous recreational facilities *(see opposite)*.

AIRPORTS *(zračna luka)*

The recently modernised **Zagreb** international airport (tel: 01-6265222, <www.zagreb-airport.hr>) is 17km (12 miles) south of the capital. It has currency-exchange offices, bars, restaurants, tourist information desks and several car-hire branches. Pleso Prijevoz (tel: 01-6331999, <www.plesoprijevoz.hr>) operate a shuttle bus between the airport and the city centre. The journey takes 30 minutes and costs 30kn. A taxi into town takes around 20 minutes; fares start at 200kn.

Croatia also has international airports at **Split** (tel: 021-203555, <www.split-airport.hr>), **Dubrovnik** (tel: 020-773377, <www.airport-dubrovnik.hr>), **Pula** (tel: 052-530105, <www.airport-pula.hr>), **Rijeka** (located on the island of Krk, tel: 051-842132, <www.rijeka-airport.hr>), **Osijek** (tel: 031-514400, <www.osijek-airport.hr>) and **Zadar** (tel: 023-205800, <www.zadar-airport.hr>).

The coastal airports at Pula, Rijeka, Zadar, Split and Dubrovnik are served by regular scheduled and budget flights, with additional routes in summer. All have currency-exchange offices, cashpoint machines, taxis and car-hire facilities. Shuttle buses are timed to coincide with flight arrivals and departures.

Where can I get a taxi?   **Gdje mogu nabaviti taksi?**

B

BICYCLE HIRE

It is relatively easy and cheap to hire a bicycle in Croatia, but congested roads and fast traffic make cycling dangerous in certain areas. The local tourist office is the best source of information about where to hire a bicycle. The Istria County Tourist Association (tel: 052-452797) has produced a detailed map of cycling routes called *Istria Bike*.

BUDGETING FOR YOUR TRIP

Compared to most western European destinations Croatia is still relatively inexpensive.

Accommodation. Hotel prices are usually quoted in euros, but you can pay in Croatian *kuna*. A double room with breakfast in a five-star hotel will cost at least 1,200kn, but you can get a comfortable room in a three-star hotel for around 600kn. Most hotels put their prices up in summer. Private accommodation costs at least 100kn per person per night, plus taxes.

Meals. For many European visitors the prices in Croatia's most expensive restaurants are surprisingly affordable. A three-course meal for two with wine in a reputable restaurant costs around 400kn. A simple lunchtime snack, such as grilled meat with bread, salad and mineral water, costs less than 100kn.

Car hire. A week's car hire will cost upwards of 2,000kn, depending on the model and the type of insurance purchased.

Nightlife. Alcoholic drinks in Croatia are reasonably priced, with a beer costing around 15kn. Hotel discos and nightclubs have small cover charges.

Incidentals. Locally organised day trips start at around 200kn. The average price for a soft drink or a small bottle of water is 10kn.

C

CAMPING

Croatia has just under 130 campsites that cater for a wide range of holidaymakers, including families and naturists. The standard of facilities is usually high, and many sites offer extensive land- and water-based sporting activities. Most campsites are only open from April to October. Overnight rates rarely exceed 140kn for two people.

Approximately 90 percent of the campsites lie along the Adriatic coast and on the surrounding islands. The best-equipped and most highly organised sites are found in the regions of Istria and Kvarner in the north. For those who really want to escape modern-day living, the most memorable sites are in Dalmatia. A total of 20 campsites are reserved for naturists. Koversada in Vrsar, Istria, claims to be the largest naturist campsite in Europe.

For a full list of Croatian campsites, plus information about each site's facilities, contact the Croatian Camping Union (Pionirska 1, Poreč; tel: 052-451324; <www.camping.hr>).

Is there a campsite near here?	**Gdje je najbliži auto-kamp?**
May we camp here?	**Je li se ovdje smije kampirati?**

CAR HIRE

International and local car-hire companies operate throughout Croatia. Drivers must be over 21 years old and have held a valid driving licence for a minimum of two years. A credit card and a current passport or national identity card are also required for car hire.

Basic insurance is included in the price, but it is advisable to purchase Collision Damage Waiver (CDW) and Theft Protection (TP) for the duration of the hire. Accidents must be reported to the police (tel: 92) immediately, otherwise the insurance is void.

A weekly economy rental (such as a Fiat Uno) starts at around 2,200kn. Bookings for major hire companies can be made on central reservation numbers or online. **Budget** (tel: 01-4805688; <www.budget.hr>), **Dollar Thrifty** (tel: 021-399000; <www.subrosa.hr>), **National** (tel: 021-399043; <www.nationalcar.hr>) and **Sixt** (tel: 01-6651599; <www.sixt.hr>) all have online booking facilities.

I'd like to rent a car	Želim iznajmiti auto
tomorrow	sutra
for one day/one week	na jedan dan/jednu sedmicu
Please include full insurance	Molim vas uključite kasko osiguranje

CLIMATE

The best time to visit Croatia is during spring and summer when days are sunny and dry. Coastal temperatures regularly reach 30°C (86°F) in August. The Croatian coast is significantly warmer than its interior. In January temperatures in the east of the country can fall as low as –1°C (30°F) but can be as high as 10°C (50°F) in Istria. Autumn, although mild, is often wet. The temperature chart that follows is for Croatia's capital city, Zagreb.

	J	F	M	A	M	J	J	A	S	O	N	D
min °C	-4	-3	2	5	9	13	15	14	11	7	3	-1
min °F	24	27	36	41	48	55	59	57	52	45	37	30
max °C	3	6	11	16	21	24	27	26	22	16	8	5
max °F	37	43	52	61	70	75	81	79	73	61	46	41

Sea temperature in Dalmatia:

	J	F	M	A	M	J	J	A	S	O	N	D
°C	13	13	13	15	17	22	23	24	22	19	16	14
°F	55	55	55	59	63	72	73	75	72	66	61	57

CLOTHING

During the peak season in July and August temperatures can exceed 30°C (86°F), making it advisable to wear light-coloured clothing in natural fibres such as cotton and silk. It is also a good idea to wear sunglasses and a sunhat, and apply sunscreen. Summer evenings are mild. Tourist venues are informal and there is no need to dress up for dinner. However, many of Croatia's twenty-something crowd and visiting Italians dress to impress at night; anyone wishing to go to fashionable bars or nightclubs would be wise to do the same.

In spring, early summer and early autumn, when the average temperatures are lower, a sweater or lightweight jacket is needed and a waterproof jacket may also be required. November to March can be cold in Croatia and a good warm winter coat is necessary.

CRIME AND SAFETY

Crime rates in Croatia are lower than those in many European countries and crimes against tourists are rare. However, as in any other country, visitors should use their common sense to help protect themselves against crime: carry personal belongings securely, do not leave valuables in unattended vehicles or on the beach and avoid walking alone at night in poorly-lit areas. Single female travellers are also relatively safe in Croatia. If you become a victim of crime call the emergency police, tel: 92.

CUSTOMS AND ENTRY REQUIREMENTS

Any foreign national entering Croatia must possess a valid passport. For stays of less than 90 days, citizens of EU countries, the USA, Canada, Australia and New Zealand can enter Croatia without a visa. South Africans need a 90-day visa to visit Croatia.

Visitors to Croatia are required to register with the local police in each town or resort that they stay in, even if visiting friends or relatives. Hotels, campsites and travel agencies offering private accommodation automatically register guests. If you fail to register you may experience difficulties if you need to report anything to the police.

The **Consular Department of the Croatian Foreign Ministry** (tel: 01-4569964, <www.mvpei.hr>) will be able to provide further information, including a list of nationalities that require a visa to enter Croatia.

Currency restrictions. Foreign currency can be taken freely into the country, but the export of *kuna* is restricted to 15,000kn.

Customs allowances. Personal possessions, 2 litres of wine, 1 litre of spirits, 60 millilitres of perfume and 200 cigarettes can be taken into Croatia without any duty being paid. Expensive items such as laptops and cameras should be reported to customs officials upon arrival to prevent problems when taking them out of the country on departure.

I've nothing to declare	Nemam ništa za prijaviti
It's for my personal use	Ovo su moje stvari

D

DRIVING

Driving in Croatia can be a trying experience. Under the former Yugoslavian government few highways were built and most roads have a single lane, including much of the main coastal road (Jadranska Magistrala) between Rijeka and Dubrovnik. New motorways have opened between Zagreb and Split, and between Zagreb and Rijeka, but traffic jams caused by slow-moving vehicles and frequent accidents remain a common problem on single lane roads.

Road conditions. Croatia's motorway network has a toll system and the roads are in a good condition. Road surfaces on many other routes are also good, with frequent passing places.

Rules and regulations. In order to drive your own vehicle in Croatia you will need a valid driving licence, registration documents and Green Card insurance. Speed limits are 50km/h (30mph) in residential areas, 80km/h (50mph) outside residential areas, 100km/h (60mph) on highways and 130km/hr (80mph) on motorways. There is zero tolerance on alcohol for drivers. It is compulsory to wear seat belts and mobile phones should not be used while driving. Headlights should be switched on at all times while driving, day and night.

The police must be informed immediately about any traffic accidents (tel: 92). Common violations such as speeding often result in an on-the-spot fine. Fines range from 300–3,000kn.

autobusna stanica	bus stop
križanje	crossroads/crossing
opasan zavoj/	dangerous bend/
opasan krivina	dangerous curve
opasnost	danger
parkiranje dozvoljeno/	parking permitted/
zabranjeno parkiranje	no parking
pažnja, radovi	men working
pješaci	pedestrians/pedestrian
slijepa ulica	no through road (dead end)
stani	halt
stop	stop
strm uspon	steep hill
vozi na desnoj/lijevoj strani	drive on the right/left
vozi oprezno	drive with care
zabranjen ulaz	no entry
zaobilaznica	detour

Are we on the right road for…?	Je li ovo cesta za…?
Fill the tank, please, with…	Napunite spremnik goriva, molim, sa…
three star/four star	tri zvijezde/četiri zvijezde
My car's broken down.	Auto mi se pokvarilo.
There's been an accident.	Dogodila se prometna nesreća.

Fuel costs. At the time of going to press petrol prices hovered around 8kn for unleaded fuel and 7kn for diesel.

Parking. Car parks, often located just outside the pedestrianised old towns, cost 4–6kn an hour. Fees are often charged 24 hours a day, seven days a week.

If you need help. The Croatian Automobile Club (Hrvatski Auto-klub – HAK) provides emergency breakdown assistance (tel: 987). Calls should be prefixed 01 if made from a mobile telephone.

Road signs. Croatian road signs generally use internationally recognised pictographs and rarely have words on them.

E

ELECTRICITY

The standard current is 220-volt, 50Hz. Plugs have two round pins.

I need an adaptor/a battery please. **Trebam adapter/bateriju.**

EMBASSIES AND CONSULATES

Zagreb is the main diplomatic base and a number of countries have embassy representatives in Split.

Australia: Centar Kaptol, Nova Ves 11/3; tel: 01-4891200; <www.auembassy.hr>

Canada: Prilaz Đure Deželića 4; tel: 01-4881200.

UK: Ivana Lučića 4; tel: 01-6009100; <www.britishembassy.gov.uk/croatia>

US:Thomasa Jeffersona 2; tel: 01-6612200; <www.usembassy.hr>.

Most embassies and consulates are open Mon–Fri 8 or 9am–4 or 5pm, and close for an hour at lunchtime.

Where's the British/ American Embassy?	**Gdje se nalazi Britanska/ Američka ambasada?**

EMERGENCIES

Police: **92**   Fire Brigade: **93**   Ambulance: **94**

G

GAY AND LESBIAN TRAVELLERS

The main religion in Croatia is Roman Catholic and, following the view of the Church, homosexuality is tolerated, but not encouraged. There are few gay venues and public displays of affection are rare. There is a limited gay scene in cities and resorts such as Zagreb, Dubrovnik, Rovinj and Hvar. For more information see <www. travel.gay.hr>.

GETTING TO CROATIA

By air. There are regular flights to Croatia from London and other European cities including Amsterdam, Berlin, Paris and Rome. Flights from outside Europe are usually routed through a major European airport such as London Heathrow. The flight time from London to Zagreb is just over two hours.

The national airline is **Croatia Airlines** (Zagreb, tel: 01-4872727; London, tel: 020-8563 0022; <www.croatiaairlines.hr>), which operates both international and domestic routes. **British Airways** (tel: 0870-850 9850; <www.ba.com>) flies from London Gatwick to Dubrovnik throughout the year. Budget airlines flying from the UK to Croatia include **Easyjet** <www.easyjet.com> from Luton to Rijeka and Gatwick to Split; **Flybe** <www.flybe.com> from Birmingham to

Dubrovnik and Split; **Ryanair** <www.ryanair.com> from Stansted to Pula and Zadar; and **Wizzair** <www.wizzair.com> from Luton to Split and Zagreb. Book online for the best deals.

By sea. Regular ferry services operate between the Italian ports of Ancona and Bari and Croatia's Adriatic coast. You are advised to book ahead in summer, especially if you are taking a car.

The ferry company **Jadrolinija** (Rijeka, tel: 051-666100; Zadar, tel: 023-254800; Split, tel: 021-338333; Dubrovnik, tel: 020-418000; <www.jadrolinija.hr>) operates services from Ancona to Split, Korčula, Stari Grad and Zadar, and from Bari to Dubrovnik, as well as a coastal ferry linking Rijeka, Split and Dubrovnik. **Blue Line** (tel: 021-352533; <www.blueline-ferries.com>) also runs ferries from Ancona to Split, Hvar and Vis. In summer, there are high-speed catamarans from Ancona to Split and Pescara to Stari Grad operated by Italian company **SNAV** <www.snav.it>, and seasonal fast ferries from Venice to the Istrian towns of Poreč, Pula and Rovinj operated by **Venezia Lines** <www.venezialines.com>.

By rail. For details of trains to Zagreb from many European cities, contact **Rail Europe**, tel: 08708 371371; <www.raileurope.co.uk>.

By bus. One of the cheapest ways to get to Croatia is by bus from London. The journey takes between 30 and 40 hours, usually with a change en route (**Eurolines**, <www.eurolines.com>).

By car. The most direct route from the United Kingdom is by motorway across Europe to Salzburg in Austria and on to Ljubljana, the capital of Slovenia, then south to Zagreb or Rijeka on the Adriatic. An alternative route is via Ancona in Italy and by ferry across the Adriatic to the Dalmatian coast *(see above)*.

GUIDES AND TOURS

Escorted coach tours are a popular way to see Croatia, as are guided walking tours of cities and towns. Local travel agents and tourist offices can arrange either of these.

Two of the biggest operators in Croatia are **Atlas** (Vukovarska 19, 20000 Dubrovnik, tel: 020-442222, <www.atlas-croatia.com>) and **Generalturist** (Praška 5, 10000 Zagreb; tel: 01-4805555, <www. generalturist.com>).

Local travel agencies can provide visitors with information about one-day or longer guided tours and excursions, as well as information on specialist activities such as shooting, fishing, climbing, horseriding and adventure sports. Atlas and Generalturist have branches thoughout the country.

| We'd like an English-speaking guide/ an English interpreter | **Željeli bi vodiča koji govori engleski/prevoditelja engleskog** |

H

HEALTH AND MEDICAL CARE

It is safe to drink tap water throughout Croatia, and visitors do not require any inoculations to travel here. The most common health problems experienced by visitors are the result of sunstroke, sunburn and dehydration, exacerbated by too much alcohol.

During summer insect repellent is recommended, as is the wearing of jelly shoes when swimming in rocky areas, due to spiny sea urchins. Contact with these is painful and requires medical attention.

Land mines were speedily removed at the end of the Homeland War by the Croatian authorities and most areas are safe, but some more remote areas around the Krajina and in eastern Croatia are still being cleared. Such areas are clearly marked.

The UK, Ireland and many European countries have an agreement with Croatia that offers their citizens free medical care. However, all visitors should take out private travel insurance to cover any unforeseen medical expenses.

Local tourist offices have lists of doctors, medical centres, hospitals, dentists and pharmacies.

Where's the nearest (all-night) pharmacy?	Gdje je najbliža apoteka (24-satna)
I need a doctor/dentist	Trebao (trebala) bih liječnika/zubara
hospital	bolnica
an upset stomach	boli me želudac
sunburn/a fever	opekotina od sunca/groznica

HOLIDAYS

The following is a list of the national holidays in Croatia:

1 January	**Nova Godina**	New Year's Day
6 January	**Sveta tri kralja**	Epiphany
1 May	**Međunarodni Praznik Rada**	Labour Day
22 June	**Dan antifašističke borbe**	Anti-Fascist Resistance Day
25 June	**Dan Državnosti**	Croatian National Day
5 August	**Dan Pobjede i Dan Domovinske Zahvalnosti**	Victory Day and National Thanksgiving Day
15 August	**Velika Gospa**	Feast of the Assumption
8 October	**Dan Nezavisnosti**	Independence Day
1 November	**Dan Svih Svetih**	All Saints' Day
25–6 December	**Božićni blagdani**	Christmas Holidays

Moveable dates:

Uskrs	Easter
Corpus Christi	Corpus Christi

L

LANGUAGE

good morning/afternoon/ evening	**dobro jutro/dan/večer**
goodbye	**do viđenja**
please	**molim**
thank you	**hvala**
Excuse me	**izvinite**
yesterday/today/tomorrow	**jučer/danas/sutra**
day/week/month/year	**dan/tjedan/mjesec/godina**
where/when/how	**gdje/kada/kako**
Is this the road to...?	**Je li ovo cesta za...?**
how long/how far?	**koliko dugo/koliko daleko?**
left/right	**lijevo/desno**
cheap/expensive	**jeftin/skup**
hot/cold/warm	**vruče/hladno/toplo**
old/new	**star/nov**
open/closed	**otvoreno/zatvoreno**
vacant/occupied	**prazan/zauzet**
early/late	**rano/kasno**
What does this mean?	**Što ovo znači?**
I don't understand	**Ne razumijem**
I don't know	**Ne znam**
Please write it down	**Možete li mi to zapisati?**
Help me, please	**Molim vas pomozite mi**
Get a doctor, quickly!	**Trebam doktora brzo!**
How do you do	**Drago mi je**
How are you?	**Kako ste?**
Very well thank you, and yourself?	**Dobro hvala, a vi?**

Days	
Sunday	nedjelja
Monday	ponedjeljak
Tuesday	utorak
Wednesday	srijeda
Thursday	četvrtak
Friday	petak
Saturday	subota
What day/date is today?	Koji je danas dan/datum?

M

MAPS

Main driving routes in Croatia are well signposted, and the free maps that are given out in tourist information centres and by car-hire companies are generally adequate. Local bookshops usually stock more detailed maps, although accompanying information is rarely in English. Maps detailing wine tours, cycle routes and walking trails are also available from local tourist offices and travel agencies in Croatia.

Good maps of Croatia available in Britain include those published by Freytag and Berndt, Mairs Geographischer Verlag, Hallway-Kümmerly and Frey. The maps vary from folded road maps to spiral bound road atlases, but most show roads, scenic routes, places of interest, national parks and ferry routes. The same publishers also produce regional maps. Kompass-Verlag publishes a detailed map of Istria with cycling routes, hiking trails and street maps. Also useful are the Insight Fleximaps to Dubrovnik and the Croatian Coast, laminated for durability and easy folding.

MEDIA

The *International Herald Tribune* and the *Guardian Europe* are the most readily available English-language newspapers. Some newsstands in major cities also stock other foreign language newspapers. *In Your Pocket Zagreb* is a somewhat irreverent local guide to the city. Published monthly, it is a good source of information for accommodation, nightlife and food. The same publisher also produces annual *In Your Pocket* guides to Dubrovnik, Osijek, Rijeka and Zadar.

The state-run television channels HRT1 and HRT2 broadcast programmes in Croatian, English and other European languages. There are also a large number of digital and satellite channels available in most hotels. The main radio stations HR1, HR2 and HR3 are also state controlled. During the tourist season Hrvatska Radio regularly broadcasts news reports, as well as reports on both road and sailing conditions, in English, German and Italian.

MONEY

Currency. The national currency is the *kuna* (abbreviated kn). The *kuna* is divided into 100 *lipa* (lp). Banknotes come in denominations of 5, 10, 20, 50, 100, 200, 500, and 1,000 *kuna* and coins are 1, 2 and 5 *kuna*, 1, 2, 5, 10, 20 and 50 *lipa*. Although the euro is not an official currency in Croatia, hotel room prices are often quoted in euros.

Currency exchange. Normal banking hours are Mon–Fri 7am–3pm and Sat 8am–2pm. Currency can also be exchanged in exchange offices, hotels and at any post office counter.

ATMs. Cashpoints are readily available and debit cards carrying the Maestro, Mastercard, Visa, Cirrus and Plus symbols are widely accepted. You will rarely find ATMs in small villages.

Credit cards. Credit card cash advances can be withdrawn from ATMs and standard international credit cards are widely accepted. Credit cards are not accepted in some of the smaller shops, hotels and restaurants.

Traveller's cheques. Euro or US dollar traveller's cheques can be exchanged at any banks and many exchange offices for a commission of up to 2 percent. You must take your passport.

Can I pay with this credit card?	Primate li kreditne kartice?
I want to change some pounds/dollars	Želim promijeniti engleske funte/američke dolare
Can you cash a travellers cheque?	Možete li mi unovčiti putni ček?
Where's the nearest bank/currency exchange office?	Gdje je najbliža banka/mjenjačnica?
How much is that?	Koliko ovo košta?

O

OPENING HOURS

Business hours are generally Mon-Fri 8am–4pm. Banks are open Mon–Fri 7am–3pm and Sat 8am–2pm. Shops and department stores in Croatia usually open Mon-Fri 8am–7pm and Sat 8am– 2pm. In the resorts shops often open Mon–Fri 8am–1pm, close for the afternoon and open again in the evening, 5–11pm.

Some larger towns have a 24-hour pharmacy and some have 24-hour grocery shops. Café-bars open Mon–Sun 7am–midnight and most restaurants open from midday to midnight. Museum opening times vary, but are generally Mon–Fri 9am–1pm or later. Some are open until 8pm in the summer. They are often closed on Monday.

Many Croatian towns and resorts have a fresh food market and a general market. These open Mon–Sat 8am–2pm; some also open Sun 8–11am. Markets selling souvenirs often have longer opening hours.

P

POLICE

Croatian police wear dark blue uniforms and are generally helpful and friendly; many speak some English.

Anyone involved in a road traffic accident is legally required to report it to the police. In the case of emergency, tel: **92**.

Where's the nearest police station?	**Gdje je najbliža policijska stanica?**
I've lost my wallet/ bag/passport	**Izgubio (izgubila) sam novčanik/ torbu/putovnicu**

POST OFFICES

Post offices are identifiable by the words Hrvatska Pošta and their yellow signs. Hrvatska Pošta provides a wide variety of services from selling stamps and exchanging foreign currency to sending faxes and telegrams. Some towns have separate post offices for handling large parcels. Post offices in cities and large towns are open Mon–Sat 7am–8pm and Sun 7am–2pm. In smaller towns the post office may close at noon while those in tourist resorts operate a split shift opening Mon–Sat 7am–1pm and Mon–Fri 5 or 7–9pm. Letterboxes are yellow and have a Hrvatska Pošta sign.

express/special delivery/ registered post	**ekspresna/specijalna dostava/ registrirana pošta**

PUBLIC TRANSPORT

Buses. Croatia has an extensive local and national bus network. Tickets for local services should be bought from the driver or at a tobacco kiosk. Services generally operate Mon–Sun 4am–11pm.

Autotrans (tel: 051-660300; <www.autotrans.hr>) is the main operator for long distance services. Tickets can be purchased from the local bus station or onboard. National bus services can be boarded at the bus stations or hailed at a designated stop. For information on long distance internal services, see <www.akz.hr>.

Taxis. Metered taxis that can be found at ranks, hailed on the street or prebooked by telephone offer poor value. A fixed-tariff list is displayed in many taxis, but it can be difficult to work out at what rate the meter is running. The starting fare is around 25kn, with each additional kilometre costing 8kn.

Trains. Rail travel is slow, with few direct connections between major towns and cities, and most Croatians do not travel by train. Tickets are cheap and can be purchased from railway stations or the onboard conductor. For train information, visit <www.hznet.hr>.

Trams. The cities of Zagreb and Osijek both have tram services that operate a similar timetable to the bus services. Tram tickets should be purchased from a tobacco kiosk and passengers have to validate tickets in the onboard machines.

By air. Regular domestic flights operated by Croatia Airlines connect Zagreb to Dubrovnik, Pula, Split and Zadar.

By ferry. Jadrolinija <www.jadrolinija.hr> is the main car and passenger ferry operator in Croatia, with numerous routes along the Dalmatian coast and between the mainland and the islands. Tickets must be purchased from the ticket office near the ferry dock prior to departure. In the summer months it is advisable to buy vehicle tickets well in advance to minimise the risk of waiting in lengthy traffic queues to board a ferry. Foot passengers can usually purchase tickets just before departure.

Where can I get a taxi?	**Gdje ima taksija?**
What's the fare to…?	**Koliko košta za…?**
When's the next bus to…?	**Kada polazi slijedeći autobus za…?**
I want a ticket to… single/return	**Želim kartu za… u jednom smjeru/povratna**
Will you tell me when to get off?	**Možete mi reći kad je moja stanica?**

R

RELIGION

The main religion of Croatia is Roman Catholic. Mass is held in Catholic cathedrals and churches throughout the country and the local tourist office will be able to advise visitors about the dates and times of local services.

T

TELEPHONES

Croatia's country code is 385. When calling from overseas the initial 0 in the local area code should not be dialled. Mobile phone numbers begin 091 or 098 and all the digits must be dialled.

Public telephones are identifiable by their blue booths. Most only accept phone cards, which can be bought from tobacco kiosks or the post office. Telephone cards *(telekarta)* cost 15–100kn depending on how many units are purchased. Direct dial international and domestic calls can also be made from larger post offices, where you pay at the end of the call.

Local, national and international calls can be made from most hotel telephones, but at a very high call rate.

Can you get me this number?	**Možete li molim vas nazvati ovaj broj?**
reverse-charge (collect) call	**naplatite osobi koju zovem**
person-to-person (personal) call	**osobni poziv**

TIME ZONES

Croatia operates GMT+1 in the winter, from October to March, and GMT+2 in the summer, from March to October.

TIPPING

Hotel and restaurant bills usually include tax and service, but it is customary to round your bill up to the nearest 10kn and to leave an extra tip for exceptional service. Taxi drivers often round up the fare or overcharge tourists, so an additional tip is not needed.

TOILETS

There are few public toilets in Croatia, making it necessary to use those in local hotels, café-bars and restaurants. If using the toilet in a café-bar it is polite to buy a drink or ask permission. The Croatian word for toilet is *toalet* – *ženski* means ladies and *muški* means gents.

TOURIST INFORMATION

The Croatia National Tourist Office (Hrvatska Turistička Zajednica) has offices in many countries. You can visit their website <www.croatia.hr>.

UK. 2 The Lanchesters, 162–164 Fulham Palace Road, London W6 9ER; tel: 020-8563 7979.
USA. Suite 4003, 350 Fifth Avenue, New York, NY 10118; tel: 212-2798672.

There are local tourist offices throughout Croatia:
Baška: Kralja Zvonimir 114; tel: 051-856817.
Bol: Porat Bolskih Pomoraca bb; tel: 021-635638.
Dubrovnik: Stradun bb; tel: 020-321561.
Grožnjan: Umberta Gorjana 3; tel: 052-776131.
Hvar: Trg Svetog Stjepana 16; tel: 021-741059.
Korčula Town: Obala Franje Tudjmana bb; tel: 020-715701.
Krk Town: Vela Placa 1; tel: 051-221414.
Makarska: Obala kralja Tomislava 16; tel: 021-616288.
Mali Lošinj: Riva Lošinjskih Kapetana 29; tel: 051-231884.

Motovun: Trg Josefa Ressela 1; tel: 052-617480.
Opatija: Nazora 3; tel: 051-271310.
Osijek: Županijska 2; tel: 031-203755.
Poreč: Zagrebačka 9; tel: 052-451293.
Pula: Forum 3; tel: 052-219197.
Rab: Trg Municipium Arbe 8; tel: 051-771111.
Rijeka: Korzo 33; tel: 051-335882.
Rovinj: Pina Budičina 12; tel: 052-811566.
Šibenik: Fausta Vrančića 18; tel: 022-214448.
Split: Peristil bb; tel: 021-345606.
Trogir: Trg Ivana Pavla II 1; tel: 021-881412.
Varaždin: Ivana Padovca 3; tel: 042-210987.
Zadar: Narodni Trg; tel: 023-316166.
Zagreb: Trg Bana Josip Jelačića 11; tel: 01-4814051.

There are also tourist offices in many of Croatia's National Parks:
Brijuni: Brijunska 10, 52212 Fazana; tel: 052-525888.
Kornati: Butina 2, 22243 Murter; tel: 022-435740.
Krka: Trg Ivana Pavla II 5, 22000 Šibenik; tel: 022-201777.
Mljet: Pristanište 2, 20226 Govedari; tel: 020-744041.
Paklenica: Dr F. Tuđmana 14a, 23244 Starigrad Paklenica; tel: 023-369202.
Plitvice National Park: 53231 Plitvicka Jezera; tel: 053-751015.
Risnjak: Bjela Voda 48, 51317 Crni Lug; tel: 051-836133.
Sjeverni North Velebit: Obala Kralja Zvonimira 6, 53270 Senj; tel: 053-884551.

WEBSITES AND INTERNET CAFES

Good websites for getting information before you go include:
<www.vlada.hr> The homepage of the Republic of Croatia contains general information about the country.

<www.croatia.hr> The Croatian National Tourist Board provides lots of useful information, with details about accommodation, transport, national parks, current events, as well as an updated weather report.
<www.visit-croatia.co.uk> Provides information about Croatia and its different regions. The site also has links to other useful websites and links to UK tour operators offering holidays in Croatia.
<www.camping.hr> The homepage of the Croatian Camping Union includes a useful contact number for prospective campers.

Internet cafés. There is at least one Internet café in most Croatian towns and resorts. During high season, opening hours are usually daily 8am–11pm. Some hotels also have 24-hour coin-operated Internet access. Rates vary according to the company providing the service and location. The local tourist office will tell you where the nearest Internet café is located.

Y

YOUTH HOSTELS

Hostels affiliated to Hostelling International are prefixed YH and can be booked via the Internet at <www.hfhs.hr>. The guide price for a bed in a six-person dormitory is 80kn; a single room is around 220kn.

YH Dubrovnik: Vinka Sagrestana 3; tel: 020-423241.
YH Krk: Dinka Vitezića 32; tel: 051-220212.
YH Pula: Zalijev Valsaline 4; tel: 052-391133.
YH Punat: Novi Put 8; tel: 051-854037.
YH Rijeka: Šetalište XIII Divizije 23; tel: 051-406420.
YH Zadar: Kneza Trpimira 76; tel: 023-331145.
YH Zagreb: Petrinjska 77; tel: 01-4841261.
YH Zlatokrila: Kaciol 26, Veli Lošinj; tel: 051-236312.
Ravnice Youth Hostel: Ravnice 1 38d, Zagreb; tel: 01-2332325.

Recommended Hotels

Until independence in 1991 large communist-era tourist resorts dominated Croatia's hotel scene. Since then, however, hotel facilities have been upgraded and there is a more diverse range of accommodation on offer, including boutique-style hotels, business-oriented accommodation and more welcoming family places to stay.

Most hotels levy a 30 percent surcharge for stays of less than 3 nights. Many hotels close between October and March, and high season rates generally apply in July and August. It is advisable to book rooms in smaller hotels in advance for summer. Most hotels accept credit cards for making reservations, but travel agencies operating as booking agents for cheaper private accommodation will usually only take cash.

Most hotels advertise prices in euros, although they expect to be paid in *kuna* (at the time of writing, €1 = 7.30kn). These price guidelines are for a double room with bath in high season, including breakfast and tax:

$$$$	over 200 euros (1,460kn)
$$$	150–200 euros (1,095–1,460kn)
$$	100–150 euros (730–1,095kn)
$	under 100 euros (730kn)

CENTRAL AND EASTERN CROATIA

ZAGREB

Best Western Hotel Astoria $$–$$$ *Petrinjska 71, 10000 Zagreb, tel: 01-4808900, fax: 01-4808908, <www.bestwestern.com>.* Located between the railway station and the main square, this hotel reopened in 2005 with a smart new interior.

Central $$ *Branimirova 3, 10000 Zagreb, tel: 01-4841122, fax: 01-4841304, <www.hotel-central.hr>.* A reliable hotel, just 100m (300ft) from the railway station, with reasonably priced rooms. Geared towards business travellers, the 79 rooms are basic but have satellite television and a minibar. Internet access is also available at the hotel.

Dubrovnik $$$ *Gajeva 1, 10000 Zagreb, tel: 01-4863555, fax: 01-4863550, <www.hotel-dubrovnik.hr>.* A stylish and upmarket hotel in the heart of Zagreb with elegant modernised guestrooms. Designer shops, trendy cafés and the city's central square are all just a few steps away.

Hotel Regent Esplanade $$$$ *Mihanovićeva 1, 10000 Zagreb, tel: 01-4566666, fax: 01-4566020, <www.theregentzagreb.com>.* One of Croatia's grandest hotels, the Esplanade used to be the rest stop for passengers on the *Orient Express*. It has a lovely art deco foyer, luxurious rooms, a health club and a casino.

Palace Hotel $$–$$$ *Trg Strossmayerov 10, 10000 Zagreb, tel: 01-4899600, fax: 01-4811358, <www.palace.hr>.* The Palace was Zagreb's first hotel and it is noted for its fine art-deco facade. All of the 126 comfortable rooms in this four-star hotel have a minibar, air-conditioning and satellite television.

OSIJEK

Hotel Osijek $$ *Šamačka 4, 31000 Osijek, tel: 031-230333, fax: 031-230444, <www.hotelosijek.hr>.* In a city with just six tourist hotels, this high-rise hotel is the best option. It is well located on the banks of the Drava River and some of the rooms provide excellent views. Facilities at the hotel include a gym, wellness centre and sauna.

PLITVICE LAKES NATIONAL PARK

Hotel Jezero $$ *Plitvice Lakes National Park, 53231, tel: 053-751400, fax 053-751600, <www.np-plitvicka-jezera.hr>.* It is well worth staying in the Plitvice Lakes National Park and this four-star hotel is the best choice. It has been extensively refurbished. Facilities include a fitness centre and sauna. Book a room with a balcony overlooking the park.

ISTRIA

MOTOVUN

Hotel Kaštel $ *Trg Andrea Antico 7, 52424 Motovun, tel: 052-681607, fax: 052-681652, <www.hotel-kastel-motovun.hr>*. This former 18th-century palace offers visitors a clean and simple place to stay. Accommodation is provided in single, double, triple and four-bedded rooms, making this a good option for families. All rooms are en suite, and many of them have outstanding views of the countryside.

NOVIGRAD

Cittar Hotel $$ *Prolaz Venezija 1, 52466 Novigrad, tel: 052-757737, fax: 052–757340, <www.cittar.hr>*. Occupying a carefully refurbished building in the old town, close to the beach and the marina, this hotel has 14 rooms and a good restaurant.

POREČ

Hotel Diamant $$$ *Brulo bb, 52440 Poreč, tel: 052-400000, fax: 052-451206, <www.riviera.hr>*. Lying a 20-minute walk east of the old town and overlooking the sea, this large, modern hotel boasts excellent facilities, including indoor and outdoor pools, tennis courts and a luxurious health and beauty centre.

Hotel Neptun $$ *Obala M. Tita 15, 52440 Poreč, tel: 052-400800, fax: 052-431351, <www.riviera.hr>*. Rooms at this early 20th-century hotel, right on the waterfront, are modern if quite small and many have balconies with sea views. The central location makes it hard to beat. Open Apr–Oct.

Hotel Poreč $$ *Rade Končara 1, 52440 Poreč, tel: 052-451811, fax: 052-451811, <www.hotelporec.com>*. Located in front of the bus station, this hotel was totally renovated in 2004 and now offers reasonably-priced, comfortable rooms as well as good sports facilities.

PULA

Hotel Scaletta $$ *Flavijevska 26, 52100 Pula, tel: 052-541025, fax: 052-540285, <www.hotel-scaletta.com>.* Close to the Roman amphitheatre, this small family-run hotel has 12 cheerfully decorated rooms and a highly-regarded restaurant.

Hotel Valsabbion $$ *Pješčana Uvala IX/26, 52100 Pula, tel: 052-218033, fax: 052-383333, <www.valsabbion.hr>.* This ultra-fashionable hotel, located on Pula's marina, has modern, tasteful rooms with air-conditioning and a minibar. The hotel also has a small pool and an award-winning restaurant.

ROVINJ

Adriatic $$ *Pino Budicin bb, 52210 Rovinj, tel: 052-815088, fax: 052-813573, <www.maistra.hr>.* Occupying an old townhouse on the central square, Adriatic has 27 well-furnished rooms, with air-conditioning, minibar, satellite television and sea views. Guest parking is provided a short walk away.

Hotel Villa Angelo D'Oro $$$$ *Via Švalba 38–42, 52210 Rovinj, tel: 052-840502, fax: 052-840111, <www.rovinj.at>.* Situated in the heart of the old town, this 17th-century former Bishop's palace has 24 stylish and spacious bedrooms that are individually furnished with antiques. The hotel garden is a hidden oasis.

KVARNER GULF

OPATIJA

Hotel Millennium and Millennium II $$$ *Maršala Tita 109, 51410 Opatija, tel: 051-202000, fax: 051-202020, <www.ugo hoteli.hr>.* Guests can choose between the main hotel and the newer annexe, Millennium II. Rooms in both hotels are classically furnished and luxurious. The hotel also has a gym, a heated outdoor pool and a seafront café.

Hotel Mozart $$$ *Maršala Tita 138, 51410 Opatija, tel: 051-718260, fax: 051-271739, <www.hotel-mozart.hr>*. This small and elegant hotel, built in the late 19th century, has just 30 guest rooms, 2 apartments and one suite. All of the rooms have twin beds (single occupancy at a reduced rate) and are light and airy, with modern bathrooms.

PAKLENICA NATIONAL PARK

Hotel Vicko $ *Jose Dokoze 20, 23244 Starigrad Paklenica, tel: 023-369304, fax: 023-369304, <www.hotel-vicko.hr>*. The Vicko is an agreeable family-run hotel with a wide range of facilities, including table-tennis. Some of the hotel rooms have sea views.

RIJEKA

Hotel Continental $ *Šetalište Andrije Kačića Miošica 1, 51000 Rijeka, tel: 051-372008, fax: 051-372009,<www.jadran-hoteli.hr>*. This pleasant two-star hotel is beside the city's canal, a 15-minute walk from town. En-suite rooms are clean and functional. The hotel has a great Internet café and also sells delicious ice cream.

Grand Hotel Bonavia $$$ *Dolac 4, 51000 Rijeka, tel: 051-357100, fax: 051-335969, <www.bonavia.hr>*. This business hotel has spacious, comfortable and classically styled rooms. It enjoys a prime location in the heart of the shopping and financial district and is easily the city's finest hotel.

THE ISLANDS

Hotel Apoksiomen $$ *Riva Lošinjskih Kapetana 1, 51550 Mali Lošinj, tel: 051-520820, fax: 051-520830, <www.apoksiomen.com>*. Located in a refurbished building in the old town, overlooking the seafront promenade, this four-star hotel has 25 rooms and one apartment, each with a marble bathroom.

Hotel Corinthia $$$ *Emila Geisticha 38, 51523 Baška, Krk, tel: 051-656111, fax: 051-856584, <www.hotelibaska.hr>*. There are in fact three Corinthia hotels, all located just metres from one of Croatia's best beaches. The completely refurbished Corinthia 1 has a three-star rating and provides the best accommodation. All of its rooms have a balcony, many of which provide sea views. The hotel also has 10 private villas, which are suitable for families.

Hotel Imperial $$ *51280 Rab, tel: 051-724008, fax: 051- 724126, <www.imperial.hr>*. Located in Rab Town's leafy park, the Imperial has light, spacious and well-furnished rooms with views over the sea or the park. Some rooms have balconies. The hotel also has three tennis courts and a mini-golf course.

DALMATIA

DUBROVNIK

Bellevue $$$$ *Pera Čingrije 7, 20000 Dubrovnik, tel: 020-330000, fax: 020-330100, <www.hotel-bellevue.hr>*. This traditional seaside hotel reopened in 2006 after total renovation as a five-star luxury boutique hotel. The spectacular cliff-top location with fine views over a tranquil bay is hard to beat.

Excelsior Hotel $$$$ *Frana Supila 12, 20000 Dubrovnik, tel: 020-353353, fax: 020-353555, <www.hotel-excelsior.hr>*. This five-star hotel has a superb position, just a 10-minute walk from Dubrovnik's old town. The rooms provide dramatic views. Guest rooms and public spaces alike are furnished to a high standard. The hotel has 18 suites, each with a jacuzzi in the bathroom.

Hotel Lapad $$ *Lapadska Obala 37, 20000 Dubrovnik, tel: 020-432922, fax: 020-417230, <www.hotel-lapad.hr>*. Overlooking Gruž harbour, 3 km from the old town, this pleasantly old-fashioned hotel has 193 rooms, and outdoor pool. A taxi boat takes guests to nearby beaches. Open Apr–Oct.

Pučić Palace $$$$ *Od Puča 1, 20000 Dubrovnik, tel: 020-326200, fax: 020-326223, <www.thepucicpalace.com>*. The Pučić Palace is one of only two hotels located within Dubrovnik's old town. A luxury hotel, occupying one of the city's old palaces off Gundulić Square, it has 19 deluxe rooms, large bathrooms and a menu of amenities, including DVD players. Very comfortable with lots of attention to detail.

Villa Dubrovnik $$$$ *Vlaha Bukovca 6, 20000 Dubrovnik, tel: 020-422933, fax: 020-423465, <www.villa-dubrovnik.hr>.* This small, upmarket hotel, with 40 rooms in a whitewashed villa and gardens overlooking the sea, has long been a favourite with fashionable visitors to Dubrovnik. The hotel has its own private beach and jetty, with shuttle boats transporting guests to the old town. Villa Dubrovnik closed for a complete renovation in 2007 and will reopen in 2008

Villa Rašica $$ *Ivanska 14, tel: 020-438 900, fax: 020-438 921, <www.villa-rasica.com>.* A one-off, this old mansion with lovely grounds sits in the verdant hills above Lapad Bay and makes you think you are in the countryside. Some rooms are in separate modern cabins. The walk to the beach is downhill. Open May–Oct.

MAKARSKA

Biokovo $$–$$$ *Kralja Tomislava bb, 21300 Makarska, tel: 021-615244, fax: 021-615081, <www.hotelbiokovo.hr>.* The Biokovo has a prime location on Makarska's seafront promenade. Rooms are smart and comfortable. Try to book a room with a sea view.

MALI STON

Vila Koruna $ *20234 Mali Ston, tel: 020-754999, fax: 020-754 642, <www.vila-koruna.hr>.* This restaurant-with-rooms provides basic but comfortable accommodation. The highlight of this peaceful location is the exquisite seafood for which Mali Ston is renowned.

ŠIBENIK

Hotel Jadran $ *Obala Tuđmana 52, 22000 Šibenik, tel: 022-242000, fax: 022-212480, <www.rivijera.hr>.* The 57 rooms in this purpose-built hotel have recently been renovated. The hotel's prime city-centre location, right on the seafront, compensates for its ugly facade and average rooms.

SPLIT

Hotel Bellevue $$ *Bana Josipa Jelačića 2, 21000 Split, tel: 021-345644, fax: 021-362383, <www.hotel-bellevue-split.hr>*. Set back from the waterfront and close to Split's most fashionable shopping street, the Bellevue enjoys a great location. The hotel has a charming exterior, which echoes its former glory, but inside, the rooms are just adequate, with no frills.

Slavija $$ *Buvinina 2, 21000 Split, tel: 021-323840, fax: 021-323868, <www.hotelslavija.com>*. This recently renovated hotel has an unbeatable location at the heart of the historic Diocletian's Palace. The hotel has 24 rooms, each with an ensuite bathroom. However, a stay here is not for everyone, as the music from the surrounding bars plays loudly until around 2am during the summer months.

Vestibul Palace $$$$ *Iza Vestibula 4, 21000 Split, tel: 021-329329, fax: 021-329333, <www.vestibulpalace.com>*. Opened in 2005, this chic boutique hotel has just 7 rooms in an old stone house near the vestibule of Diocletian's Palace. Polished wood, glass and natural light blend with Roman stone walls to create an intriguing mix of ancient and modern. Definitely the top place to stay in the heart of the city.

TROGIR

Hotel Fontana $$ *Obrov 1, 21220 Trogir, tel: 021-885744, fax: 021-885755, <www.fontana-commerce.t-com.hr>*. This is a well-equipped and comfortable hotel in the heart of the medieval town. The hotel apartment, with its own kitchen, lounge area with sofa beds, Jacuzzi and a master bedroom, is a good option for families. The hotel also has a good restaurant, with tables out of doors on a sea-facing terrace on summer evenings.

ZADAR

Hotel Kolovare $$ *Bože Peričića 14, 23000 Zadar, tel: 023- 203200, fax: 023-203300, <www.hotel-kolovare.com>.* The Kolovare is just a 10-minute walk from the old town and also close to the beach. There are 235 smart rooms, plus a heated outdoor pool and sun terrace.

THE ISLANDS

Hotel Kaštil $$ *Frane Radiča 1, 21420 Bol, Brač, tel: 021-635995, fax: 021-635997, <www.kastil.hr>.* Overlooking the harbour, this old stone building has 32 smart rooms with minimalist style furnishing, plus a restaurant and lively cocktail bar.

Hotel Korčula $$$ *Obala Tuđmana 5, 20260 Korčula, tel: 020-711078, fax: 020-711746, <www.korcula-hotels.com>.* Overlooking the seafront promenade in the old town, this was Korčula's first hotel when it opened here in 1912. There are 20 basic but comfortable rooms and a pleasant terrace restaurant and café.

Hotel Pod Stine $$ *Pod Stine, 21450 Hvar, tel: 021-740400, fax: 021-470499, <www.podstine.com>.* This hotel has a peaceful seafront location just 15 minutes walk from Hvar Town. It has 40 comfortable rooms and a four-bedroom apartment that is ideal for families. The hotel also has a private beach, arboretum and restaurant.

Hotel Restaurant Paula $$ *Petra Hektorovića 2, 21480 Vis, tel: 021-711362, fax: 021-711362, <www.hotelpaula.com>.* The Paula is a small and friendly hotel located in historic Kut. The en-suite rooms are spacious and comfortable and some have a sea view. The hotel also has an excellent seafood restaurant.

Riva $$$$ *Riva, 21450 Hvar, tel: 021-750100, fax: 021-750101, <www.suncanihvar.com/riva>.* The 100-year-old Hotel Slavija, situated right on Hvar's waterfront promenade, was given a makeover in 2006 and reopened as the ultra-fashionable Riva 'yacht harbour hotel', with contemporary design, a trendy bar and nightclub, and the Roots restaurant offering creative Mediterranean cuisine.

Recommended Restaurants

Croatia has a wealth of dining options, from stylish, expensive restaurants and fine-dining hotel eateries to fast-food outlets and more relaxed establishments specialising in seafood or hearty meat dishes that are typical of the Croatian hinterland. Most restaurants open daily from midday to midnight. Each region in Croatia has its own culinary specialities. Along the coast fish forms a huge part of the staple diet, whilst inland roast lamb and roast suckling pig feature. For details of local specialities, see page 95.

The prices indicated are for a starter, main course and dessert with wine, per person. Prices usually include tax and a service charge. However, if service has been good it is customary to round the bill up to the nearest 10kn. More expensive restaurants accept major credit cards, but it is not wise to assume that they all do. Fast food places and cheaper eateries usually don't accept credit cards.

$$$$	over 300kn
$$$	200–300kn
$$	100–200kn
$	under 100kn

CENTRAL AND EASTERN CROATIA

ZAGREB

Baltazar $$$ *Nova Ves 4, 10000 Zagreb, tel: 01-4666808, <www.restoran-baltazar.hr>*. Barbecued meats served in a rustic dining room in winter and in a courtyard garden in summer. Situated in Gornji Grad, close to the cathedral. Closed Sun.

Paviljon $$$$ *Trg Kralja Tomislava 22, 10000 Zagreb, tel: 01-4813066, <www.restaurant-paviljon.com>*. Open Mon–Sat for lunch and dinner. This elegant restaurant, located in a picturesque park, is perfect for celebrating a special occasion. Local chef Stanko Erceg creates exquisite dishes that draw on Croatia's finest ingredients. His signature dish is crispy roast duck on a bed of red cabbage and figs. The restaurant is a favoured haunt of Croatia's celebrities, politicians and diplomats.

Pod Gričkim Topom $$$ *Zakmardijeve Stube 5, 10000 Zagreb, tel: 01-4833607*. Up in Gornji Grad, near the funicular station, this informal restaurant serves up Dalmatian meat and fish specialities, and also offers fantastic views over the city. Closed Sun evening.

OSIJEK

Slavonska Kuća $$ *Kamila Firingera 26, 31000 Osijek, tel: 031-369955*. Open daily for lunch and dinner. A traditional Slavonian restaurant in the historic Tvrđa, renowned for its spicy fish stew.

VARAŽDIN

Pivnica Raj $ *Ivana Gundulića 11, 42000 Varaždin, tel: 042-213146*. Open daily for dinner and until 1am on Saturdays. This lively beer hall has a hearty and extensive meat-based menu.

THE KVARNER GULF

OPATIJA

Le Mandrać $$$ *Obala Frana Supila 10, Volosko, 51410 Opatija, tel: 051-701357, <www.lemandrac.com>*. Bosnian chef Deniz Zembo does sublime things with seafood at this new-wave Croatian restaurant, situated at the end of the Lungomare promenade beside the fishing harbour at Volosko.

THE ISLANDS

Konoba Rab $$$ *Kneza Branimira 3, 51280 Rab, tel: 051-725666*. In the old town, this old-fashioned restaurant serves tasty meat and fish dishes in a cosy dining room on two levels. Ask to try *rapska torta* (Rab cake, a local speciality made from almonds) for dessert.

Nada $$$ *Ulica Glavača 22, 51516 Vrbnik, Krk, tel: 051-857065, <www.nada-vrbnik.hr>*. This highly regarded restaurant serves local meat and fish specialities on a large terrace in the old town. Be sure to try the local Žlahtina white wine, which you can also buy here in presentation boxes to take home. Open daily Mar–Oct.

Pizzeria Draga $$ *Braće Vidulića 77, 51550 Mali Lošinj, tel: 051-231132*. Lošinj's favourite pizzeria serves pizza, pasta and salads on a large covered terrace just one block back from the harbour.

ISTRIA

POREČ

Barilla Pizzeria $$ *Eufrazijeva 26, 52440 Poreč, tel: 052-452742*. This traditional Italian-style pizzeria serves up tasty pasta and pizza dishes on a lively terrace in one of Poreč's most beautiful squares.

Peterokatna Kula $$$ *Decumanus 1, 52440 Poreč, tel: 052-451378*. Located in a refurbished 15th-century tower, this sophisticated restaurant serves up carefully prepared Istrian specialities.

PULA

Restaurant Valsabbion $$$$ *Pješčana Uvala IX/26, 52100 Pula, tel: 052-218033, <www.valsabbion.hr>*. Open daily for lunch and dinner. An award-winning restaurant fusing Istrian and international influences, with an emphasis on presentation and service.

ROVINJ

Al Gastaldo $$$ *Iza Kasarne 14, 52210 Rovinj, tel: 052-814109*. Open daily for lunch and dinner. This cosy restaurant serves Italian and Istrian dishes. The beefsteak with truffles is recommended.

Giannino $$ *Via A. Ferri, 38, 52210 Rovinj, tel: 052 813402*. Open daily for lunch and dinner. Giannino serves first-rate fish. It is located in a secluded street away from the main tourist area.

DALMATIA

DUBROVNIK

Lokanda Peskarija $$ *Na Ponti bb, 20000 Dubrovnik, tel: 020-324750.* Situated next to the covered fish market in an atmospheric setting overlooking the old harbour, this informal restaurant serves excellent seafood. Very popular with locals, so reservations are essential for dinner.

Orhan $$$$ *Od Tabakarije 1, 20000 Dubrovnik, tel: 020-414183, <www.restaurant-orhan.com>.* Open Feb–Oct. Just outside the city walls, close to Pile Gate, Orhan serves up Dalmatian seafood dishes at outdoor tables overlooking the sea.

Sesame $$$ *Dante Alighieria bb, 20000 Dubrovnik, tel: 020-412910, <www.sesame.hr>.* Open daily for lunch and dinner. This taverna near the Pile gate serves local specialities such as seafood risotto.

MALI STON

Vila Koruna $$$ *20234 Mali Ston, tel: 020-754999, fax 020-754 642, <www.vila-koruna.hr>.* Open daily for lunch and dinner. This is an excellent fish restaurant and the conservatory is a perfect setting.

MAKARSKA

Stari Mlin $$$ *Prosvibanjska 43, 21300 Makarska, tel: 021-611509.* Colourful paintings, candles and incense set the mood in this old stone building with a vine-covered terrace. The menu is rather special – Dalmatian seafood dishes plus select Thai specialities.

ŠIBENIK

Gradska Vijecnica $$$ *Trg Republike Hrvatske 3, 22000 Šibenik, tel: 022-213605.* Outdoor tables at this elegant restaurant (formerly the town hall) have stunning views of the cathedral.

SPLIT

Adriana $$ *Obala Hrvatskog narodnog preporoda 6, 21000 Split, tel: 021-344079*. This large, brash seafront restaurant and pizzeria may appear rather a tourist-trap, but the food is tasty and there's a good view over the port. Locals love it, despite the surly waiters.

Kod Jose $$$ *Sredmanuška 4, 21000 Split, tel: 021-347397*. All a *konoba* should have: flag-stone floor, wooden furniture, great barbecued fish and an endless supply of local wine served by candlelight.

TROGIR

Restoran Fontana $$$ *Obrov 1, 21220 Trogir, tel: 021-884811*. Open daily for lunch and dinner. Fresh fish and pizza.

ZADAR

Fosa $$ *23000 Zadar, tel: 023-314421*. Open daily for lunch and dinner. Good fish restaurant located in the former customs house. Enjoy a fish platter or spaghetti with clams.

THE ISLANDS

Adio Mare $$ *Svetog Roka bb, 20260 Korčula, tel: 020-711253*. Open Apr–Oct for dinner only. A real gem hidden in a narrow side street in the old town. Serves typical Balkan meat and fish dishes.

Bounty $$ *Riva bb, 21450 Hvar, tel: 021-742565*. Open daily for lunch and dinner. Serves delicious grilled fish.

Macondo $$$$ *21450 Hvar, tel: 021-742850*. Open daily for lunch and dinner. One of Hvar's best restaurants, situated in a narrow street set back from the main square.

Villa Kaliopa $$$$ *V. Nazora 32. 21480 Vis, tel: 021-711755*. Open daily for dinner in summer. Romantic setting in the garden of a Renaissance villa. No real menu, just a choice of superb fish. Cash only.

INDEX

Berlitz pocket guide
Croatia

Second Edition 2008
Written by Robin McKelvie
Updated by Tony Kelly
Managing Editor: Dorothy Stannard
Series Editor: Tony Halliday

Photography credits
All photography by Gregory Wrona
except: AFP 21; akg-images London 18;
Jon Buckle/Empics 22; Hrvatski Povijesni Muzej,
Zagreb 16; Robin McKelvie 91; Mark Read 12,
27, 29, 30, 32, 51, 66, 87, 89, 95, 96, 99, 100;
Trip/M Barlow 36/37.

Cover picture: Fantuz Olimpio/4Corners

All Rights Reserved
© 2008 Berlitz Publishing/Apa
Publications GmbH & Co. Verlag KG,
Singapore Branch, Singapore

Printed in Singapore by Insight Print
Services (Pte) Ltd, 38 Joo Koon Road,
Singapore 628990. Tel: (65) 6865-1600.
Fax: (65) 6861-6438

Berlitz Trademark Reg. U.S. Patent Office
and other countries. Marca Registrada

Every effort has been made to provide
accurate information in this publication,
but changes are inevitable. The publisher
cannot be responsible for any resulting
loss, inconvenience or injury.

Contact us

At Berlitz we strive to keep our guides as
accurate and up to date as possible, but if you
find anything that has changed, or if you have
any suggestions on ways to improve this guide,
then we would be delighted to hear from you.

Berlitz Publishing, PO Box 7910,
London SE1 1WF, England.
fax: (44) 20 7403 0290
email: berlitz@apaguide.co.uk
www.berlitzpublishing.com